From Me To You

Ala Yvonne (Kinlow) Corbin

From Me To You
by Ala Yvonne (Kinlow) Corbin

Printed in the United States of America

ISBN 978-1-60647-932-2

www.xulonpress.com

Preface

It's been about twenty years since Yvonne, five other friends and I got together for weekly Bible study and prayer. I wanted to read through the Bible in a year, but I didn't think I'd achieve that goal on my own. I called my Spirit led, prayer-loving friends to help me. We experienced God together during those studies. He spoke to us and through us. Sometimes He gave us glimpses into our futures.

It was Yvonne I saw with my eyes closed during one of our prayers. She was walking down a sidewalk, carrying a briefcase. When I opened my eyes to tell everyone what I saw, God gave me words to speak directly to Yvonne. She was going to be traveling- carrying God's Word (since then she's ministered in and out of the state of Washington). He also told her that she would write a book. Writing a book wasn't on Yvonne's to-do list; she was surprised by what God gave me to say to her.

Twenty years ago, I was excited for Yvonne because God was going to bless her to write a book. Today, I'm excited for you, the readers, because God is going to minister to so many of you through **From Me To You**, that God-inspired book. I wanted to read through the Bible in a year, but I didn't think I could do it alone. My friends gladly helped and I (we) did it! If you're feeling like you're battling life alone and like you're about to lose, DON'T GIVE UP. Think of the people in this book as your friends coming from different places to help you win your God-ordained victory and to show you their battle scars. There are stories to remind you that although people go through terrible things, they can come out "better, not bitter". My story is among them in 'Give Love Away'.

—Ruth Russell
Writing Consultant

Yvonne, your bravery and ability to articulate events that have been unpleasant and uncomfortable but real is incredible. Life has many transitions, and you have had your share. Some challenges could have been devastating but you are a conqueror, displaying faith that is undaunted, unwavering and you are succeeding.

From Me To You is an account of real life experiences. Many of the episodes I can affirm with mixed emotions and thankfulness.

You are a star that shines in a many dark nights. Nobody promised us that life was going to be a rose garden, but through the many midnights you are a shining jewel.

Yvonne, my sister, thanks for sharing a life full of crossroads. God has been faithful and your resilience is impressive.

From me to you- Victories bring joy and gracious moments. The night is passed, enjoy today.

—Your brother, Ezra
Pastor of Holy Temple COGIC
Spokane, WA

From Me To You is truthfully real life; not only told but as seen.

> — Sarah Davis, a blood-bought sister,
> a student of the world and life observer.

I am blessed to call Yvonne Corbin my friend. We have walked together, prayed together and worked together for several years. And yes, even cried together. Yvonne is very gifted and anointed in her ability to share with women and to reach into their lives and bring life, hope and change. She is able to share with women on deep personal levels because of her God given gift and because of what she has walked through as a daughter, wife and mother.

You will be blessed with what she shares in this book and it will inspire you to keep on trusting God because He never fails us regardless of circumstances that come our way in life.

He is always faithful.

> — Jacque Simmons
> Pastor of Women's Ministry
> Trinity Church, Tacoma, WA

I have been so blessed to have met Yvonne a few years ago. I admired her from afar before the Lord opened a door for us to get together. Our pastor mentioned that she was writing a book. Since I had assisted in the editing of some books for Youth Pastors at my former church in Texas, I approached Yvonne and offered my services. Yvonne and I prayed about it and she graciously allowed me access to her life.

What an honor it has been to get to know her and be able to call her friend. Her life is a clear example of growth in Christ—of trials, persecutions and health attacks—when she refused to lay down and give up! Rather, she focused even more on her relationship with Christ and became a mighty woman of God as a result.

From Me To You is a book that will make you laugh, make you cry, make you take a look at your life and see ways to overcome your own circumstances through the Lord.

—Joan LaReva
Friend and Editor

Table of Contents

My Acknowledgements

Many, many thanks to my parents, Reverend Ezra Dewitt and Mary Kinlow, who gave me such a rich heritage. They are resting in their heavenly home where they laid up many treasures as they displayed their love and commitment to Christ and each other in every aspect of daily living in our home.

My husband, Roy. Make no mistake, you are my hero. When needed, you are by my side. Other times you are behind me pushing. I'm most grateful for the times you are ahead of me, leading the way, always praying for and loving me. You have never denied who I am. I thank God for you.

My four children. Each one of you is a blessing from God and I thank Him for who you are and for how you have inspired and supported me in this writing and the many seasons of my life. We are fa-m-ily.

To my family, friends and associates, I acknowledge you for each part you have played in my life. All of your support, your mentoring, your prayers, your encouragement and your words of wisdom have been a continual charge for my mental and spiritual battery.

To you who accepted me for being who I was…who I am.

And to you who accepted me for who I was but encouraged and allowed me the space to become who God intends me to be. I especially acknowledge and thank each of you who have a glimpse of me in the Spirit realm and continue to encourage and nudge me forward and upward.

To you, who have been thorns in my rose bush, thank you. Without those interruptions my emotional and spiritual muscles, strength and stamina would not be what they are today. And many experiences and words in this book would not have been possible. My testimony would not be as strong and the vision of God's glory would not be as bright.

To you, my new found Christian family. Thank you for accepting me with a fragile heart, for strengthening that which remained and for speaking to the Spirit within me. Your faith and trust in me and more so, the God in me is very profound. It has surged me forward.

To each of you who help to make this book a reality... the word spoken into my loins, the many confirmations that were given along the way; the proofreaders, the consultants, the editors, the publishers.

I thank God for planning my destiny before I was in my mother's womb. And for not giving up on me when it seems like I, like Jonah, run in the other direction.

Thank You, God, for Your faithfulness. I only ask for grace to trust You more.

Dedication

This book is dedicated to "you," the reader, to encourage you to confront every circumstance that may come your way and inspire you to continue to reach for your highest level of potential.

Life is a journey with many different scenic spots. Where there are mountains, God gives us the strength to climb, and for valleys He provides steppingstones to mount up. When He shows us the way through many different viewpoints or windows, it is up to us to make the choices and the changes. That can be difficult because there is fear in change. Sometimes it is just making the decision to get started. And usually once we decide to lean into and meet head-on the circumstance, we'll come in contact with someone else who is going through the same situation or someone who has had similar experiences. We then realize that God has provided a human commonness with whom we can gain insight, encouragement and strength for the task.

My prayer is that as you read these pages you will access with boldness and confidence the power that is available to us through Christ Jesus our Lord. And that your inner man will be strengthened with might through His Spirit. Be assured that there really is good in the midst of the bad and the ugly. Dwell in HIS presence.

YOU ARE NOT ALONE!

We are a Body, your pain is mine and I share mine with you and together we can find comfort in the comfort of God, " Who comforteth us in all our tribulation, that we may be able to comfort them which are in any trouble, by the comfort wherewith we ourselves are comforted of God" (2 Corinthians 1: 4).

BE BLESSED!!

Introduction

God has many ways of encouraging us to continue to pursue the destiny that He has ordained for us. Just like He designed the many seasons and changes in nature, He also knew that there would be many transitions in this journey called "life." Therefore, in His love for us, He devised a plan that would make our path easier. Not only did He send His Son, Jesus to die for our sins, the Word for us to read and His Spirit to empower us, He allows us to experience seasons and transitions so that we may share our pain and growth process with others.

I have been so blessed to experience strength and encouragement by many testimonies that I have heard from others, by word of mouth and by reading. It is my endeavor to share with you some of the seasons that God has walked me through in hopes that you will find the comfort in knowing that where ever you are right now, it is only a season and God is there to walk with you through it, to the other side.

It was not easy being a PK (pastor's kid) or being the youngest of 11 children. I got married and left home at the age of seventeen. Not only did I leave home but my husband and I moved from Arkansas to Washington State within three months after we were married. I can recall dreaming at night that *"tomorrow I'm going to visit Mama"* only to wake up and realize I was thousands of miles away. I had to learn early to trust in the God of my parents and soon come to know Him in a very real way for myself. It was approximately three years before I saw my parents after our move.

At times when I thought my life was coming together for smooth sailing, something would happen and a strong wind of life would occur and knock me off course.

Although I had heard and accepted the call of God for ministry, it was after my mom's death that I felt God impressing upon my heart to share some of my pain and traumatic experiences through outreach and later through writing.

Not only do I share many of my hurtful times, I share with you my main Source of survival and choices that I have had to make to maintain my stance. Don't allow yourself to be weary in your journey because there is peace to be sought and found in the midst of any storm.

In the Dedication to this book, 2 Corinthians 1: 4 is taken from the King James Version. Let me now share that same passage from the Amplified version (verses 3 and 4): "Blessed be the God and Father of our Lord Jesus Christ, the Father of sympathy (pity and mercy) and the God [who is the Source] of every comfort (consolation and encouragement). Who comforts (consoles and encourages) us in every trouble (calamity and affliction), so that we may also be able to comfort (console and encourage) those who are in any kind of trouble *or* distress, with the comfort (consolation and encouragement) with which we ourselves are comforted (consoled and encouraged) by God."

This text *is* a source of help to me during the times when God sets me apart. It helps me to accept the troubles that come my way and to know that God has a dual purpose- to strengthen me and to increase the depth of my testimony. It is an inspiration in helping me to share with you the pages of this book.

God is of no respecter of persons, as He has been and is with me, so will He be with you. He is the Creator of this journey call life but the quality of it is an individual choice. If we take too many detours or stay too long at any *scenic spot,* we can easily lose focus and take longer in reaching our destiny, if we reach it at all.

This book is complied of many facets of my life's experiences in short story form. Whether you read it as a devotional, an inspirational or just leisure reading, I pray that you will be encouraged to know that God is the balancer, the common denominator and the stabilizer in all of life's circumstances and situations. I hope that you will be as blessed reading them as I have been in writing them.

All is Well

All being well is not based on every
"i" being dotted
and every "t" being crossed;
but that God sent His Son, Jesus,
who came and gave His life on Calvary
that we may live.

All being well is not that there is no pain,
no disappointments, or no shame,
for that is not why Christ came;
but that through Him, amid the struggles
the dilemmas and the transitions,
eternal glory can be our gain.

The Voice of Silence

Listen to the silence
Listen through the silence
Listen for the silence

Speak Silence Speak

Speak through the heart beat
Speak through the heart ache
Speak through the heart break.
Speak Silence Speak

Speak and I will hear
Speak and I will know
Speak and I will follow
Speak silence speak as I listen
Listen…
Listen…..
Listen…..

Marriage — For Better or Worse

Even thou the traditional marriage vows end with " 'till death do we part," we often find that many who perform the ceremony, along with family and friends who attend, have already said within themselves, *"This one won't last. Just wait until the honeymoon is over."* What an atmosphere to begin a lifetime journey!

I was in 7th grade when I first met Roy. He was in the 9th grade. We attended the same school. This is how we met. A friend and I were hall monitors. One day we were asked to take a note to the Agriculture class. The teacher was not in the classroom and when we walked in, Roy ran up to the front of the class, grabbed me and kissed me (no, it was not on my cheek)! I was surprised and embarrassed. However, I did kiss him back! My friend, who liked Roy, was jealous and told the principal. Roy and I were called into the principal's office where we were scolded, then spanked!

That was the beginning of our secret relationship. We kept our relationship secret because I was 12 and not old enough to date.

When I did turn 16, I was not allowed to date Roy because we were from different religious backgrounds. I was raised in a traditional, Pentecostal family. My dad was a Pastor.

Roy was raised in a traditional Baptist home with a single mom. Now can you better understand why our relationship had to remain secret? For five years we had to be satisfied seeing each other at school, or the grocery store where Roy worked. I loved the times when Roy walked me home from school.

However, Roy graduated two years before me, so it became more difficult to see each other. The front of their house faced the back of our house. There was an alley alongside their house that came to the front of our street. Our house was the second house from the alley and our back porch faced the alley. From our porch I had a clear view of the alley. People used the yard next to ours as a shortcut to get to the alley, and often this was an opportunity for Roy and me to see each other.

Even talking on the phone was a challenge. There was one phone in my house and it was near the chair my dad loved to sit in. When I talked on the phone, my dad, Papa as we called him, would say, "Who you talkin'to?" And after what seemed like only a minute, "Been on the phone long 'enough. Hang up." God forbid the times when Papa answered the phone and Roy was calling me. Papa's answer was "no" more than it was "yes." I would know that it was Roy and when I got the chance, I would sneak and call him back. Sometimes when the phone rang and no one was on the other end, I would go outside to see if Roy was close by.

Every now and then, we would see each other when I walked to my older sister's house about two blocks from us. Other times we would sneak and see each other at a friend's house who lived close to my sister. Although we cared deeply for each other, our relationship was expressed through hugging, kissing and petting each other. However, when things are done in secret, the forbidden fruit becomes more luscious and passions get harder to control.

As we grew older and became more aware of our sensuality, our relationship developed into a more intimate one. We began to talk of spending the rest of our lives together. But when passions are high and body parts are exposed to each other, penetration is not necessary for conception to take place. Sperm travels swiftly and if it is a monthly ovulation time, the egg is very receptive. Pregnancy can result, and in my case, did. So although I was pregnant when we got married, it was not the result of penetrating sexual intercourse.

Note of caution to the young-in-love and to parents: clear sexual education is very important. We were not told this. All the girls were ever told was "keep your panties up and your dress down." The young men were told to "keep your pants zipped up." Yes, doing that was the perfect solution, but life, emotions and passion cause many unwise decisions in moments of excitement. And unfortunately for us, we did not share this information with our own children until it was much too late (you'll understand this later).

It wasn't easy being a pregnant teenager of one of the most prominent families in our hometown, especially in those days. My father was a pastor and felt compelled to walk in honesty. It was just a little while before graduation when he told the principal of our school that I was pregnant and guess what? Although I was not showing and was in the top percentage of my class, I was not allowed to walk sown the aisle in my cap and gown to receive my diploma with my classmates.

People began to say why I wasn't going to walk down the aisle. The principal used this as an opportunity to bring attention to this well-known and respected *family of God*. This was one of the best scandals in our hometown and people were curious as to what we were going to do. Some were upset with the principal and others were disappointed that my dad had revealed our situation.

So, on May 20, 1966, in my older sister's living room with her husband officiating, our moms, one of Roy's brothers and my sister's children as witnesses, Roy and I were married. Our marriage was a choice of our love and was not by force.

One of my older brothers and his wife, who were familiar with the circumstances, offered to adopt the child or to care for him or her until I had furthered my education and was ready to assume this responsibility. With either of those choices I could be in the child's life. But if I remember correctly, if we chose either of these options, Roy and I could not continue with our relationship.

Because of Roy's family history and having been separated from his dad, he wanted to be in his child's life and being a responsible mature person, he asked me to marry him. I said yes. After all, we were in love and had been for five years.

Three months after we were married, we moved to Washington state with one of my brothers and his family and have made our home here since then. We knew it wouldn't be easy, but we focused on the love that we had shared for the past five years instead of the negatives.

We encountered many obstacles here. Although we were young, we, shall I say Roy, was already a man and he jumped right into the role of a godly husband by becoming my "head" or "covering" in every aspect. We stayed with my brother and his family for approximately four months. Roy and my brother carpooled to work and his wife and I shared household duties. However, on Sundays, Roy and I attended different churches, according to our different denominations. This pattern continued for about eight years, during the time that we had all four of our children – 1 son and 3 daughters.

Looking back, it was a Holy Spirit moment when I decided to check out Roy's church. Imagine my surprise when a lady at the church revealed to me her intentions to pursue Roy for her own. She saw him as a good father, a deacon and a godly man who sang in the choir. To her, he appeared to have an unbelieving wife-she'd never seen me there before. Just in the nick of time! Thank you, Jesus.

I was also aware that I needed Roy to be visible with me in my church circle. When there were state-wide meetings, Roy usually kept the children while I was gone. I began to get flirtatious comments and glances from the male membership. As Roy and I discussed these issues, we began to participate more in each other's church settings. About 10 years into our marriage, we began to attend the same church.

Roy was a good provider and we talked, shared and made decisions that were good for us and did not ask for or always follow advice given by others. We were not mere "yes" people. We had our own mind and made our own way.

Meanwhile on the old home front, no matter how much changed, some things stayed the same. Fifteen years after our marriage, while visiting in our hometown, an older member of my husband's family told me, "After all these years, I guess I might as well accept you as a member of this family." I can't describe the inner disruptions that took place, but having been taught to respect my elders, I decided then that getting others' approval was no longer a major factor. I would always respect them but I would do what was best for my husband and me. We reached the point where we had to make a decision to *somewhat* put our upbringing aside and focus on the Word of God. We finally decided together that we would go forward and make our own family traditions.

In 1986 our life became a real battleground. When the enemy realized that he could not destroy us through temptations, criticisms, opinions of others or other negatives, he turned toward our children, our health and our financial security.

One of our smart, destine-to-succeed teenage daughters became pregnant in her junior year of high school. Once again, I felt as if all eyes were on us. The circumstances of Roy's and my marriage were not a big secret. When people learned of our daughter's pregnancy, their opinion seemed to be, *"The sins of the parents follow with the children."* I could feel them watching us. Now the question is their eyes was *"How will they handle this?"* I found myself challenged by many things. Any experience of unwed pregnancy is difficult, but it is especially difficult when it's a teenage pregnancy.

When I first suspected that she might be pregnant because of her demeanor, she said there was no way she could be pregnant because she had not had sex. When we took a home pregnancy test and it was positive, she was in disbelief. And so was I After much detailed conversation, there was no doubt of the way she had conceived- de`ja`vu.

During her pregnancy, I recall times when I tried to avoid being seen in public with her. Not because I didn't love her, but more because I did not want her exposed to other people's judgments. At church, I would try to be in a crowed space so that there would be no room for her, only to have someone else relinquish their seat for her. I was confronted with inner emotions that were difficult to face.

Many times when parents have overcome past failures, we put them in the sea of forgetfulness and fail to allow God to show us signs, warnings and applications that we need to share with our children as we walk in forgiveness and mercy. We forget that the enemy is shrewd and although we are under grace, he plans for us to live in generational failures-if we allow him to. It is never easy to face one's self in the mirror. But when I recognized my pride and my guilt, I gave it to God and I became her covering. We talked, we cried, we forgave each other. We talked. We cried. Oh, did I say we cried? We did! I wonder if maybe that is one of the reasons God allowed her a second chance-because of our acceptance, her repentance and our covering over her.

The young man's parents seemed so unreasonable to us. They had no tolerance for this unwed pregnancy. They are prominent leaders in a religious Pentecostal denomination. They spoke many accusations against our daughter and she was mostly blamed. Their son was not mature enough to take his responsibility as the father of the child. His parents insisted on a paternity test, which we agreed to give them, along with a suit against their son declaring statutory rape. He was of age, she wasn't. Roy and I believed that scripturally we should first try to settle the dispute among ourselves and not go through the law (1 Corinthians 6). So we scheduled a meeting with the young man, his parents and our pastor. However, neither the boy nor his parents showed up or called to cancel. They remained unavailable throughout the pregnancy.

Three weeks after our grandson was born, Roy was in a life threatening accident. Roy worked the swing shift as lead man at a beverage-distributing warehouse in Tacoma, Washington. On July 28, 1987 as he was retrieving articles from underneath a loading ramp, one of his co-workers suddenly backed onto the ramp, causing it to slam down violently, crushing Roy underneath. If Roy had failed to leave the beveled lip of the loading ram extended as he went beneath the dock (preventing it from lowering completely), he would never have survived.

Roy knew he was in trouble and just fell on his knees and cried, "Lord, help me." His co-workers freaked out and he had to tell them to call 911 first and then whoever else. Paramedics responding to the call were amazed that he never lost consciousness throughtout the ordeal. Because his injuries were so severe, hospital ER staff expected him to die at any minute, so he was left virtually unattended through most of the night.

Roy's head and back were traumatically injured. His face was so mangled from the blade of the loading ramp lid, that his left eye and socket were literally scooped from his face. His right eye was so damaged that the doctors expected he would be blind in that eye. His face would require major reconstruction, which the doctors hesitated to begin because they had no hope that he would survive. But they didn't know about Roy's God and the prayers of many believers and friends in his behalf.

Because the doctors did not know what Roy had looked like before this accident, they said they would do the best they could to reconstruct his face, but they could not promise me anything, other than to tell me, "He may look like a monster *if* he survives."

I'll never forget that night! That phone call changed my life forever. I was at a church social function when our daughter called me and said, "Dad's boss called and said he is being taken to St. Joseph's Hospital. You need to meet them there immediately." I didn't know what to expect, but on my way out of the door I told someone in passing of the call and said that I would call back when I got to the hospital.

When I called back to the church and said that it was critical, many people from church came to the hospital for support. One of the men who came worked in the medical field in the military, understood the terminology and had an understanding of just how critical Roy's situation was. He and a few others went back to church and held an all night prayer vigil. We are forever grateful to them. The word spread quickly and we had the prayers and support of many family, friends and well wishers from all over the country.

When a family friend from the valley came and heard the report, he immediately took me home to get a picture of Roy and returned to the hospital. Photo in hand, he banged on the steel surgical door until he was heard! He provided the surgeons with what was needed to reconstruct Roy's face. Thanks be to God!

The next morning when the surgery was over, with a hugely swollen head, bandages and tubes, I could still see an old scar on Roy's nose and he was able to talk with me. the prognosis now was favorable.

Our family was placed in counseling soon after the accident because the prognosis for families surviving that kind of trauma is not good. After a few sessions of going separately and together, the counselor said that we had the potential to survive because of our strong faith, strong sense of family and family support.

About a month into Roy's recovery, a nurse friend of mine called to see how things were going. I had just given Roy a dose of one of the prescribed medications and I began to tell her about it. She remained very calm as I spoke, but told me later that inwardly she was alarmed. Within minutes after our telephone conversation, she was standing at my door. If it had not been for her I can only imagine what would have happened to Roy. When I showed her the medicine and the dosage that I had given Roy, she immediately made a phone call to Group Health (where she was employed). They told her to get Roy to the nearest hospital ASAP! It wasn't just a matter of Roy needing to have his stomach pumped because of over medication-it was actually a matter of life or death.

The accumulated dosage of Dilantin I was giving Roy was enough to kill an elephant! Roy's mouth was wired shut and his face was pinned together underneath his skin from his original surgery. Even after the ER doctors cut the wires, Roy still could not open his mouth. The doctors had to pry it open enough to insert a tube in his mouth and down his throat. Charcoal needed to be pumped into his stomach to dilute the medicine and make him regurgitate. After much caution and care on the part of the medical staff, and with the power of intercessory prayer, I was able to take my husband home again to continue his recovery. Another move of God.

The following morning I was awakened by the sounds of panic coming from my daughter's room upstairs. Our seven week old grandson, Antowne, had been found lifeless by his mother. I reacted quickly with CPR, and he lived on life support for four days. During those days, God gave us time to resolve within ourselves to let His will be done. It was very difficult, especially for Roy, because he was with our daughter when the baby was born and had had time to bond with him.

My inner self often cried out, *Enough already*, but God proved over and over that His strength is made perfect in weakness. You see, Roy had to under-go several more surgeries. In the midst of fighting for his health, we were in constant legal battles for financial support through Social Security and L&I. You would think that with his injuries having occurred at work, his work record and the fact that he had a family, it would be an automatic monthly check, at least a supplement. But no. If we had not had some financial investments, we would have gone under.

In the fall of 1989, I started college to maintain a positive focus while making continual adjustments to my family life. Little did I know this was the beginning of a new season for me. Our eldest daughter was married and living in Germany, our second daughter was away in college, our son was in the military and our youngest daughter was the only one still at home. My need was to keep sane while she went through puberty and my husband was dealing with the life changes he had to encounter. Our youngest child had seen her dad be a very positive influence in her siblings' lives, but he was not able to do so with her because of his changed temperament as a result of his trauma.

Whereas Roy had always been mild mannered and even tempered, after the accident, he became unpredictable. He would shift to being angry and hostile to being withdrawn and depressed. When our older children were going through puberty, Roy had spent quality time with them individually at their place of choice. There he would listen and walk through the situation with them.

But with our youngest, following the accident Roy was impatient and intolerant. This was a very challenging time for all of us. Sometimes I intervened in her behalf when I felt he was being too strong. Looking back, I feel this probably did her more harm than good.

Previously, Roy and I had always had a united front. Now things were different. And yet there were times when my patience with her was worn down. Instead of being thankful for my leniency and becoming more responsible, she took it as an opportunity to be more adamant about doing her own thing. Consequently, one Christmas, while our oldest child was in Germany, we bought airline tickets for the other two sisters to spend the holiday there. As much as it hurt, the decision to keep our youngest daughter home seemed to be the right step at the time.

I understood much of the turmoil that she was going through because I was the only child at home during my high school years. I knew the loneliness of being raised in a strict home and church environment while facing the challenges of society and peer pressure.

In February, 1990, I was diagnosed with chemical-induced asthma and was advised to find another profession. As the operator/owner of a beauty salon, the atmosphere there was the contributing factor to the asthma. It took me several months to confront and deal with the diagnosis and the prognosis for my life.

I was without any other skill and my business was the steady income that kept our heads above water. We had one daughter in college, the youngest one was in high school and

I had recently started college myself. Can you even imagine the pressure???

One day I heard the Lord ask, *Is it harder for Me to keep you healthy until you have a new career and your girls have finished school or for Me to supply you with your financial needs?* As I meditated on that, the Lord already had another angle in motion that would push us into a decision.

In December 1991, I had to have major surgery. After much analyzing and prayer, my husband and I decided that I would not go back to work. What sense did it make to rearrange my clients for two months while I recovered from surgery, then return to work for another few months only to leave the business? It seemed reasonable to just make a clean exit. I also could hear the voice of God assuring me that if He had intended for me to handle all of this on my own, He would have taken Roy to be with Him at the time of the accident. Roy was still here with me, he was still my head and the way by which God would, as He always had, supply the needs of our family. Thus began our new walk with God...

It would have been easier if Roy's medical and legal situations were all settled. But instead of things getting better, it seemed as though they were getting worse. There was always something else that we had to deal with. I remember once when our daughter was on her way home from college on summer break, her car broke down in Moses Lake. Roy went to get her and his car broke down in Vantage. I was home and the car I was driving quit on me. Enough...enough...enough already...!!!

How could we go forward when the past (and the present) just couldn't seem to be resolved? We wondered, *Why is it so hard and why does it take so long for the worldly system that we put our trust in and paid into for so long to come to our aid? Why were they so insensitive and unsupportive? How much of this is because Roy looked big and robust? Was it because he is Black? What is God saying in all of this?* We didn't believe that God was allowing those things to happen to make us bitter, indifferent and/or underprivileged. It was just that somewhere, in the midst of all the painful drama, **we were missing it.**

I use the word drama because it seemed as though we were on center stage and all eyes were on us. One of my employees would tell me how people would ask her if I was really okay! God was my hiding place and if you didn't know the road I was traveling, you wouldn't have known it by looking at me nor by being in my presence. For I had learned to dwell in my secret closet and to worship the Almighty.

However, one of those not-so-good- times is very vivid in my mind. I had recently returned from the funeral of my oldest sister and many of my emotions were harried. I can't remember what set me off. I just remember that I reached out and totally cleared a wall in my house that was the picturesque of our travels. I was so distraught that with one scoop of my hand I smashed many cups and plates that had been collected during our travels. When it seemed like *Mr. Roy* was not sensing my need, I proceeded with one yank to snatch the glass shower door off its hinges.

I then left the house in a half-crazed fog walking. Someone who knew me drove pass then turned around to talk with me. She asked how I was doing. I told her I was having a mental breakdown. Her reply was, "Saints don't have breakdowns." I said, *Yes they do and I was having one. The difference was I know it and am doing something about it.*

She took me to her house for a few hours where I found some peace and quiet, which allowed me to be myself again. After she brought me home, I had to clean up my mess. You know, it's no fun to make a mess in a fit of rage and then have to do the clean-up! I thank God for His faithful because He helped me through that period and strengthened my inner man. Not only was I grieving for my sister, that was the beginning of my grieving the lost of my husband as I had known him and the start of accepting who he was and what God was allowing to happen in our lives.

I saw us as being on stage since we were married and I felt that it was time to draw the curtains or at least have an intermission break.

You see, every day life doesn't stop because of unexpected interruptions! God spoke to me that if I would keep my focus on Him, as others are looking at me (us), they would see His reflection. I'm reminded of portion of a church pledge.. "to be a representative of holiness in my every day life and that my life will be a mirror that reflect the image of Christ."

What a tremendous task. Sometimes I made it and other times I didn't. When I didn't make it, I leaned on the shoulder of those whom God placed in my life and went deeper into my secret closet. One day I actually went into my walk-in closet with a stool and just sat in the dark, seeking the presence of God. He was there.

Roy was constantly being re-evaluated. And each time he would be sent to a new team of professionals. This caused our healing wounds to be ripped open all over again as we were required to retell the incident. You would think that since they had the file before them, they could read for themselves. But no, we always had to start from beginning to end, again, and again and again. This always caused a major emotional set back. Yet, it was one of God's ways of getting us to deal with unresolved anger.

After a while I began to look at things differently. I began to think that each time we were sent to a different medical team and evaluations board, there were people whom God wanted to hear and see of His power firsthand. That changed my attitude. I would no longer be angry as we sat in front of the many different teams of physicians, but I began to speak more of the miracle God created in Roy. I was able to then encourage my husband to look at this dilemma from another angle. No matter what we were confronted with, and yes, it was from the hand of the enemy, but God allowed it. And since God doesn't put more on us than we can bear, we would be okay. This new attitude allowed God more freedom to bring His purpose to the forefront.

In the midst of the many, many challenges we faced, we were determined to remain faithful and loyal to our God and family. We made a pack early in our marriage that separation was never an option; we would always remain together and work through whatever problems occurred.

I'm thankful that we were recommended for counseling and it was beneficial. We were there for approximately three years. We had to go through the cycle of grief. Although Roy was still alive, we had to release the visions and goals we had planned for our family. We needed to accept who Roy now was and allow God to show us how to move forward in spite of these changes.

We also had to grieve the death of our first grand child. Maybe I should say that before we could fully accept the pregnancy and how it affected the family, we had to grieve the lost. I'm pleased to see how we have survived.

It was not easy for our daughter to go back to school with the many questions of her peers…"What did you have, a boy or girl? What's his name? Who baby-sits while you're at school?" Questions, questions, question-a constant reminder of her lost. Yet, she completed high school, received a scholarship and finished her four-year college with a degree in accounting. Tremendous healing has taken place between us and the paternal family of Antwon. We, the grandparents, refer to each other as "friend." Antown's dad calls me "Grandma." "After all," he says "I made you grandma first."

In the midst of one of our greatest transitions, my husband said to me "I thought we said for better or for worse!" That statement pricked my heart. Although I was not at a point of wanting out of the marriage, it moved me to take another look at my level of commitment and my inner response to any and every situation.

Commitment is vital. "'Till death do we part," is a powerful concept. Sometimes death is a welcome possibility, and the challenge of how do we live until we die, is a big hurdle that must be overcome. It does not matter who is better or who is worse. We realized we are no longer "twain" but **one**. When we touch and agree, God is in the mix and with Him all things are possible.

It isn't always easy because more times than not, it seems that the burden of emotional and spiritual stability is on the wife. And for me, especially since Roy's accident in '87, I've had to focus and refocus on how God ministered to me before the accident and just know that He is faithful and His Word is true.

You see, the accident happened on Tuesday evening. But the Monday night before that, God ministered to me through one of my church sisters at a women's meeting. She stated that she could see the Lord holding me in His arms and just rocking me. With that, she took me in her arms and as I laid on her shoulder, without understanding why, I began to weep and the weep turned into a deep inward moan, which erupted into uncontrollable tears. God was allowing me to grieve **before** the accident because He knew I would need all of my strength to deal with the care of my family. John 16:33 was a verse given to me, *"These things I have spoken unto you that in Me ye might have peace. In the world ye shall have tribulations: but be of good cheer; I have overcome the world."*

There are many times when it would be easier to give up because life isn't always fair, but as I look a little closer, I know that God didn't bring me (us) this far to leave us. And when I see the character of my "love" (Roy), who he is and his love for God, his love and commitment to me and our family, I continue to **choose** the godly way because nothing can happen to me that God and I, along with Roy, can't handle.

I often refer back to the verses of scripture that God gave me at the onset of Roy's accident from Psalm 91: 15,16- *He shall call upon me and I will be with him in trouble; I will deliver him and honour him. With long life will I satisfy him and shew him my salvation.* And of course, John 16: 33.

This is an ongoing choice and each time I choose yes, I find new ways to convey my love to him and I see how God really is in the midst of it. As I choose to be strong in the Lord and in the power of His might, my whole being aligns with His.

Is it a struggle? Yes. Sometimes it could be as simple as not looking at the situation, but knowing the heart of your spouse. The scripture says that two are better than one, and it takes one of each kind to make a whole.

Differences attract and when they are used to compliment each other and not to compete, the outcome can be a wonderful testimony of who God is. It is a matter of keeping in mind that there will always be things that irritate each of us about the other. Is it in an instant? No. Waiting is hard. But when the choice is made to submit to God, we recognize that God sees and feels everything we do. He is our High Priest and when we touch and agree, we can have anything we ask of the Father in Jesus' name because His plans for us are peace and to bring us to an expected end.

I'm aware now more than ever of the reality of Romans 8:28, "And we know that all things work together for good to them that love God, to them who are the called according to His purpose."

Even when storms keep on raging in my life and it's difficult to distinguish from which source they are coming, I rest assured that God will lead me to my place of destiny as I keep my focus on Him. And when I come out on the other side my soul will be anchored and I will shine with the glory of the Lord.

The Corbin Family does have a testimony to share. As Roy, our children and I meet people in our everyday lives, we can be more sensitive and compassionate with where other people are, and we can share words of encouragement from our heart to theirs.

Although we have had many obstacles, I'm glad to say that they did not become barriers or roadblocks, but steppingstones to complete our destiny.

Our family may be scattered in three different states now, yet God had given us a closeness that is wonderful. What's more important is that we are all Believers in committed relationships with Jesus Christ. We all belong to Christian fellowships where we are accountable, nurtured and responsible.

Roy and me together "till death do we part for better **and** for worse!
Together for 42 years and counting!

Resurrection Day

As I get older I find that the Easter celebration has more and more meaning for me. Each year I try to see which one of the last seven sayings of Jesus has greater impact on my life than the year before.

Easter is a time when I think of new beginnings. Restoration. Revitalization. Even though we are encouraged to be content in whatsoever state we are in, to be thankful for what we have (know how to adapt and not let our surroundings dictate our attitude and relationship with God), I feel that we should continue to reach above, beyond and within to find new life and new hope until Jesus' return.

This year I have a new outlook on "It is finished." (John 19:30) Jesus really did finish the struggle between heaven and hell. He showed us how to end each challenge that we face by saying, "into thine hands I commend my spirit." (Luke 23:46) When Jesus finished His mission, everything that needed to be done to insure our journey from earth to heaven was accomplished. He had borne the pain, shame, rejection and temptations that would be stumbling blocks in our path.

We do not have to bear our infirmities or weaknesses alone. Not only did He bear our *griefs,* (Isaiah 53:4) He also left us a road map—The Word—and the Holy Spirit to dwell within us to comfort and guide us.

Jesus spent many hours with His disciples and the multitudes sharing with them His mission and how to maintain focus in the midst of challenges. He showed them how to go to the Father for reinforcement, how to be alone and how to fight the adversary. In John 16:33, He left these words for our encouragement, comfort and reassurance: "These things I have spoken unto you, that in me ye might have peace. In the world ye shall have tribulation: but be of good cheer; I have overcome the world."

In the 17th chapter of John, Jesus was so concerned that all who come to the Father would remain in Him through relationship, that He prayed for us in advance. Although we are in this world we are not of the world and He asked His Father to keep us from evil and to sanctify us through His word.

Now the choice is up to us. Will we follow in His steps all the way and commend our spirit to the Father? Or will we try to succeed on our own?

The Father is a gentleman and will not force us against our will. He will not commit spiritual rape. We must surrender to Him as Jesus did. Jesus said in John 10:17b, 18a: "...I lay down my life, that I might take it again. No man taketh it from me, but I lay it down of myself."

We have the promise that the same power that raised Jesus from the dead will also "quicken our mortal bodies" (Romans 8:11) and we, too, will rise again.

But until that day, whenever we are in a dilemma or a transition and don't know what to do or which way to go, we need to remind ourselves that Jesus took the keys of hell and death (Revelation 1:18). As we commend our spirit to the Father, as we submit our will to His and say "nevertheless, Thy will be done," (Luke 22:42) to Him, He will give us renewed strength, restore our courage, rejuvenate and refresh us in Him until He comes to carry us home.

When an inward change takes place and our heart says "Yes, Lord," the struggle is not as great from that point to the moment when we have our breakthrough—it's just a matter of time.

Resurrection Day (commonly known as Easter) is not only one Sunday in a year, but *resurrection day* can occur any time and all the time. When we think all hope is gone, whether for a wayward child, an estranged spouse, a negative health prognosis or a financial crisis, God can step in. And in the nick of time, everything is changed. Many times there might not be an immediate change in the situation, but our perspective and our attitude changes. Then we receive new revelation, new insight and our spirits become revived.

Thus, happy Resurrection Day!

God's Easy Living

In all thy ways acknowledge him, and He shall direct thy paths. *Proverbs 3:6*

In spite of the many changes life brings, we really can live in peace. God is not influenced by circumstances. His promises remain constant regardless of the situation. So why then, is today a day of disorder, chaos and depression?

The prayer comes to mind that reads, "Dear Lord, so far today, I am doing all right. I have not gossiped, lost my temper, been greedy, grumpy, nasty, selfish or self-indulgent. I have not whined, complained, cursed or eaten any chocolate. I have charged nothing on my credit card. But I will be getting out of bed in a minute, and I think that I will really need your help then." (Author unknown)

Knowing that the status of today is not a negative on God's part, I must look within myself and see where the lack is. Could it be that I simply didn't choose my path today? I said by my actions that whatever happens, happens and I will roll with the punches. I didn't pray. I didn't acknowledge God. I just went about my day as if I were in control of it all. And only when I encountered a negative interruption, did I stop and consider how I began my day. Even though I may have hurriedly overlooked the Almighty One, when I stop and consider my ways, He is so faithful to come to my rescue and supply my need.

On tomorrow, while everything is perfect, before I get out of bed, I will choose my path. I will honor this day that the Lord has made and ask Him to order my steps. I will put on His whole armor and when I feel the pressure of the day, I will draw nearer to Him, submit to Him and be strong in His power and in His might.

I realize that this is not done before I step out of bed at the beginning of the week only, but each day and throughout the day as the need arises.

I choose to use the authority and power that God has made accessible to me through the Holy Spirit and rest in His care, for it is in Him I live, I move and I have my being (Acts 17:28).

Easy living does not mean that everything is always okay; it simply means that I choose to put my trust in God knowing that He has ordained my life from beginning to the end even before it began. And with the challenges and the struggles, God has already prepared a way of escape for me.

I learn to not judge, criticize, lay guilt or blame on anyone or any circumstance, no matter how distasteful it may be. Instead, I *choose* to rest in the Lord and wait for His directions. And while I'm waiting, I do not doubt. I learn to observe and enjoy my surroundings in the waiting room. There may not be magazines, TV or games in the waiting room, but there are people to fellowship with and to exchange life stories, places to visit and new things to experience…in the waiting room of life!

Just like He gave the children of Israel manna from heaven each day (Exodus 16:15), He told us in the Lord's Prayer to pray Give us this day our daily bread (Matthew 6:11) and I have found that when I do as the Israelites did and gather each day my manna, my food from God through

His Word, prayer, praise and worship, He makes my path bearable.

Yes, the storms will continue to rage and the tumults of life will continue to come, but when your soul is anchored in the Lord, you will not give in to the temptations of life and life will be easy (easier).

To live in peace is not to have any negative experiences, but it is confidence in knowing and in resting in the character and the Word of God.

Looking unto Jesus the author and finisher of our faith; who for the joy that was set before him endured the cross, despising the shame, and is set down at the right hand of the throne of God. (Hebrews 12:2)

Points to ponder...

- Have I claimed the faith and trust as Paul did in 2 Timothy 1:12b and say, "I...am persuaded that he is able to keep that which I have committed unto Him...?"
- Have I committed, entrusted (am I sure He is able to guard) my all to Him until the day He returns?
- Am I truly convinced that God is all-powerful and all-knowing and that He is the end and the middle as well as the beginning?
- Do I only trust Him when things are going well and I can see my way?

In The Meantime

Have you found that waiting is one of the hardest things in the world for you to do? It is like being told, "I have already bought your gift, *but* I'm not giving it to you until..."

You go to the doctor and he tells you that you are finally pregnant. But you have to wait for another three months before you know if it's a boy or girl, then another six months before you can see and hold him or her. What do you do in the *meantime*, the in-between time?

You get a word from God and it is just what you need. But what happens between the time you are given the word and the time it comes to fruition? You wait...and wait...and wait.

On one of my daily calendars, I once read, "God makes a promise—faith believes it, hope anticipates it, *(but in the meantime)* patience quietly awaits it."

I remember reading a book by Joyce Meyer entitled, "Enjoying Where You Are on the Way to Where You're Going." The essence of that book is to realize that life is a journey, a process, and the enjoyment of life is not based upon all enjoyable circumstances. But the attitude we have during the process will determine our outlook, the time span and the lessons learned.

I think of the scripture texts, "But godliness with contentment is great gain" (I Timothy 6:6) and "...for I have *learned,* in whatsoever state I am, therewith to be content." (Philippians 4:11) Learning contentment, how to cope and how to maintain a life of peace in the midst of storms is a process.

I have found that when an unpleasant situation arises in my life, God has already given me a warning. It is up to me to go "back to the future" in order to determine my course of action.

In the Word of God we are told to "...bless the Lord at all times..." (Psalm 34:1) and "In every thing give thanks: for this is the will of God...concerning you." (I Thessalonians 5:18) There are also songs that ring loud with peace in the midst of the storm. Words to one are. "I have good days; I have bad days. My good days outweigh my bad days. I won't complain because my soul is anchored in the Lord."

But how does one get from the situation to the praise, and what do we do in the meantime?

I think of the four lepers in the Old Testament (II Kings 7:3) who were sitting outside of the gate, waiting to die, when they finally said, "Why sit we here until we die?" Since for them death was inevitable, they decided to take a chance and go into the enemy's camp. They found unexpected things on the other side. In the meantime, while waiting to die, they decided to move forward and go into the camp, and in that process, they found life.

I have found that there are two sides of life for me (and many angles on both sides). From 1987 to 2001, I was the caregiver to my husband who had been seriously injured in an industrial accident. The waiting was difficult, but I was not immobile. However, in August of 2001, I became the patient. I was immobile and many times frustrated.

From August of 2001 through February of 2002, I only had the use of one of my arms. I had a viral infection that affected my right arm from August to October. As I was recuperating from that, while on vacation at a conference in Florida, I fell and broke my left hand in three places. As it would be, I couldn't have surgery on my hand for three weeks because of a death in my family and I had to travel to Arkansas. Upon returning, I found my doctor was gone for a week. Then three weeks after the surgery, my therapist noticed that one of my fingers was not rotating properly and would require another surgery. Yet that surgery could not take place for another five weeks because it was too soon to go back into the incision. Exactly two months and two days later, I had the second surgery.

In the meantime, what was I to do? How could I handle the time line during transitions?

I am a person who is always on the move. I'm active in my church, a volunteer at our hospital, and a substitute schoolteacher in addition to my role as homemaker. How was I to fulfill all my roles with one arm? What was I supposed to do to fill my time and keep my sanity?

I reflected. As I go back in my mind, I'm reminded of the many times God has sent a word to me that I'm to write a book. Well, you guessed it! In the meantime, while I'm waiting for full recovery, I'm writing this book.

In the meantime **I waited**. Waiting is never easy. When we learn to wait, we also learn to wait with patience and quietness. That means no complaining. We learn the art of delayed gratification. We learn contentment—to be happy and satisfied with whatever we have, wherever we are.

While I waited, **I listened** to what I heard and to what I did not hear. I recall the passage of scripture when Elijah was hiding because Jezebel was seeking to kill him. He listened for God in the wind. He wasn't there. In the earthquake, He wasn't there. In the fire, He wasn't there. But in a still small voice he heard the message from God. (I Kings 19:11,12) So even as I listen, I have to still my mind and my emotions.

I can be in my secret closet all closed in with God, but yet continue to do my daily tasks. Because the listening I am speaking of, is the listening with my heart and my spirit. An interesting thing about listening is that we can even listen in our sleep. In the Bible, we read of how God spoke through dreams and visions and He still does today.

Listening can also be heard through songs, through prophets, pastors, and teachers. These pastors and teachers can be in our local church or in the media. When listening, it must be done with careful insight from the Holy Spirit. The good must be taken in and the other be blown away into the wind. I receive the good in the name of a prophet knowing that I will receive a prophet's reward.

I once read in a woman's inspirational journal that if we would stop talking long enough to listen, we could learn something. For it is only in silence that what we hear, we can filter from our head into our heart. In silence can we hear the heartbeat of God and His still, small voice. In quiet, we realize spiritual insights that reach far beyond words.

I reevaluated who I am. Is what I'm going through a part of making me into who I am supposed to be? Will this help me to reach another level of whom God thought I would be when He first thought of me? Am I who I say I am? Is this who I want to be or am I trying to be who someone else says I should be? I once heard a man say that we spend much time trying to please people whom we don't even like. Why?!

I listen for the voice of God to confirm that this book is of Him and not of people's opinions.

I confessed and repented. Not that I was committing any known sins, but I acknowledged my humanness and my dependence on God. I repented of anything and everything as it was brought to my attention when I prayed, so it would not affect my attitude, causing me to build walls and withdraw.

I forgave. It is so easy to explain, justify and ratio-nalize a hurt, but there is so much freedom in just forgiving.

Forgiveness is a choice, and as I chose to forgive and release the situation to God, I positioned myself in a place where God can move more rapidly in bringing *it* to pass. When I forgive, I open the door to new revelations and growth within my own life.

I reconfirmed Whose I am. I began to remember the character of God, "He is not a man that He should lie..." (Numbers 23:19) I re-affirmed my belief that He knew me before I was formed in my mother's womb and that the plans He has for me have not changed, no matter what the circumstances may be. He is still bringing me to my expected end. (Jeremiah 29:11)

I prioritized. I took a closer look at what I expected of me, what *humans* expected of me and most of all what God expects of me. I learned to say no. I learned to say no and not feel guilty.

I read. I read God's Word; especially the Word that He has given to me when I've needed it most. I go back and study it and find the correlation of how it applied to my present situation and discovered tools to make it applicable in my everyday life. I read related books; in particular, those that are Christian based. I read my journal and revisited the things I've experienced, how I handled them and what God spoke to me during those seasons.

I did outreach. When I get busy interceding for others, I lose sight of me, myself and I. I uplift others by praying for them—telephoning them and praying with them. A visit by mail and in person, when possible, is wonderful. I reach out beyond myself and how I feel to accommodate someone else. Proverbs 11:25 reads, "The liberal soul shall be made fat: and he that watereth shall be watered also himself."

I became impatient. Many times in my impatience, I become frustrated and that leads to anger. The anger takes me back to my secret closet only to discover that that just may be the reason why God allowed this to happen—to let me see myself and that human part that has not been broken and surrendered to Him.

I cried. Sometimes the tears are because of anguish and sometimes they are of joy. But it does not matter because I know that weeping is only for a season and "They that sow in tears shall reap in joy. He that goeth forth and weepeth, bearing precious seed, shall doubtless come again with rejoicing, bringing his sheaves with him." (Psalm 126:5, 6)

I fought. The fight is not in the physical but in the emotions and in the spirit realm. Even though I know that Jesus has already won the war, I must show up to fight in every battle. It is the continual struggle between good and evil, right and wrong. However, the fight is not as having no hope and without God. (Ephesians 2:12) The struggles that we face must be confronted until Jesus returns to gather us home.

I rested. Resting isn't always an easy thing to do. In the flesh, I want what I want, when I want it, like I want it…NOW. Psalm 37:7 encourages us to rest in the Lord and wait patiently for Him. In Psalm 16:9b it says, "…my flesh also shall rest in hope." The Amplified version reads, "…my body too shall rest *and* confidently dwell in safety." Resting doesn't mean that I just sit in my chair or lie in my bed and sleep. It refers to being free from worry, to be at ease and to have peace of mind. Therefore in resting, I am silent before the Lord. I don't tell Him how nor when to do *it,* I trust Him and yes, when the night comes, I lay my body down and sleep and my sleep is sweet because I know and trust the One who neither sleeps nor slumbers.

In the meantime, as I am waiting for God to bring to fruition those things that have been declared for me in my life, **I grew**—sometimes without even recognizing it. When I listen to myself as I speak to others, I can hear the promises of God being spoken out of my mouth with boldness and power. I feel the assurance on the inside that the Holy One *is* with me. Neither circumstances nor my attitude can change His love or His end for me. They may have been interrupted, altered or delayed, but not canceled.

It is important that we don't think we've made it when we see growth strides because there is a testing time.

As I was getting back into the full swing of things following those two surgeries, I had to have yet another surgery on my hand in September of 2003. So you see, the *meantime* is ever with us and how we respond during that time is crucial to the next phase of our life. What is learned will help boost us to the next level in our journey.

I've learned that I do have direct access to God anytime and anywhere I need Him. Through Him I really am more than a conqueror.

My sights are not on the visible, but faith based on the eternal. I know that I can trust *my* God. (Did you notice that I said "my" God?) You see, by now I know that He really is mine. We have developed a relationship and I am convinced that He will never leave me nor forsake me. I am assured that He has my best interests at heart. When I leave this earthly place, I know I have a building not made by hand.

So what happens in the meantime? I will **praise** and **worship** my God for He is worthy of all my praise. I resolve like David in Psalm 34:1, "I will bless the Lord at all times: His praise shall continually be in my mouth." I will worship and bow down, I will kneel before the Lord *my* Maker. (Psalm 95:6) Psalm 146:2, "While I live will I praise the Lord: I will sing praises unto my God while I have *any* being." I will continue to "...Lift up mine eyes to the hills, from whence cometh my help" (knowing) "my help cometh from the Lord..." (Psalm 121:1) and "I will praise thee (God) with my whole heart: before the gods will I sing praise unto thee (Him). I will worship toward thy holy temple, and praise thy name for thy lovingkindness and for thy truth: for thou hast magnified thy word above thy name." (Psalm 138:2)

I wondered (I speculated, I thought), **I pondered** (mulled over, thought about, gave consideration to) **I meditated** (turned over in my mind).

All of the things I do, do not happen in any set order and not all of them on the same battlefront. It isn't always as easy as 1,2, 3 because many times there will be struggles.

However, I've learned that the four D's I was taught when I went to college: Decision, Devotion, Dedication and Determination are factors in how long the *meantime* is and if the outcome will be positive or negative.

I've also learned that the meantime could actually be a "mean" time—a time when it seems that nothing is going right. A time span where it seems that all things are standing still in the midst of horror. It could be a nasty, appalling and awful phase of life with financial disaster, health issues, relationships severed or altered, reputations scarred, or employment changes, and sometimes, death. Yet during this time as well, we must learn that the "mean" time is also a bridge for us to cross in order to reach our expected end. It is just a season! In spite of it all, pressing toward the mark is still in focus.

In *everything* I will continue to pursue God. I will lift up holy hands without wrath and doubting. (I Timothy 2:8) I will offer the *sacrifice* of praise. (Hebrews 13:15) I will keep my focus on Jesus, the Author and Finisher of *my* faith. (Hebrews 12:2)

Letting Go

As I get older, I realize that there is an art to *letting go*, and that it is easier said than done. Especially of people and things that we hold dear and that we claim as ours.

I've often heard and read the words "let go" but in my adding the *ing*, I'm stating that it is a continual process that is learned as we go.

To let go is to give a free rein of operation to…and that is scary! As humans, we have a fear of the unknown. We like to feel like we are in control. However, when we let go and let God, the process is not as traumatic. It is no longer free rein to anything or anyone, but it is giving control to God, the One who knows all about the situation and has our best interests at heart—trusting in Him no matter what happens. The more we know of God, His character and His Word, the sooner and easier it is to let go.

I think the letting go process begins when we send our first child off to kindergarten (or the baby-sitter if we work). But because it is a normal routine, we hardly notice that the process has begun. We continue to let go when our children begin to date, go away to college, choose a career and get married.

Yet, I find that there is another kind of letting go and it is the releasing of *my* methods, *my* timing, *my* opinions and *my* unsolicited advice. (Many of "my" thoughts and actions are because of the traditions I've been schooled in most of my life). It is when the children are allowed to choose who they date, where they go to college, who they marry, where they will live and yes, when and how many children they will have, without stipulations.

Now don't misunderstand me, traditions are great because through traditions we establish customs that identify who we are in our ethnicity as well as family. As we spend time with family and friends, we learn to love, understand, appreciate and value God and His creation, who we are as individuals and what His purpose is for us.

I also believe that we must begin to alter our traditions to best fit our individual family needs and to the times in which we live. A note of caution though, we must *never* alter the Law of God nor His principles. I believe that we should have a clear understanding of the principles by which the tradition was established. My husband and I have different religious upbringings, but the foundation and godly principles are the same. Therefore, we chose to release many of our individual family beliefs and to establish ones for our immediate family that still stood on a solid but Biblical foundation.

I'm reminded of a story I heard once that involved four generations of women. The youngest daughter wanted to know why the ends of the ham were always cut off before being baked. When the oldest mother was asked why, it was because she did not have a dish large enough to fit the ham in so she cut it off to fit. Can you imagine!!!

One of my great on-going challenges is to refrain from releasing some motherly advice to my grown children (unless I'm asked.) When a need to let go is evident, it is human to feel like we are losing control, that we have not done or taught enough of the *right thing*. Our sense of connection is lost and feelings of rejection emerge. These feelings of rejection can easily lead one to be withdrawn.

As I get older, I have stopped resisting the process. I withdraw just far enough and long enough to evaluate the situation, admit my feelings (whether they are valid or not) and reaffirm my faith in God. As I let go, I rest more in God and realize that all things do work together for good. I see that the principles that we taught our children are very much intact and that they are becoming who God has designed them to be. They were not mine to own and keep anyway! They were just entrusted to my care for a while. I was to be the bridge that connects them to meet and become acquainted with God and to develop their own relationship with Him. God has ownership—He only gave me stewardship.

The more I relax and release to God, the more peaceful I become and it's easier to know that God is bringing me *and* all that concerns me to the destiny He has promised.

A friend of mine once told me of a book entitled, "Hold Me While You Let Me Go." I let go by giving them the okay to make their own choices and decisions; I hold them by loving them and lifting them up to God through prayer and intercession, knowing that He's in charge.

Although the empty nest syndrome is facing us all, I've discovered that when it looks like the door is closed, as I chose to release the my, my, mys, I find that I have much more. Not only do I have the children to whom I gave birth, I also have within these children friends, confidants and people in whom I can trust and depend.

Not only is it difficult to let go of things in the natural, but sometimes even more so in the spiritual. When we have been accustomed to doing things a certain way, being with a certain group of people, worshipping in a certain style, how can it possibly be God when someone receives a revelation to fellowship and build relationships with others who are different than what we are familiar with!!! It is so easy for us to quote scripture verses like, God is doing a new thing, There is one body and one Spirit...one Lord, one faith, one baptism...one God and Father of us all... But when something is done out of the norm, it can't possibly be of God! This is the way it's always been done! And this is what you've been taught all your life! We often fail to look at and understand other portions of verses like, one body...many parts...fitly joined together.

May I say that letting go is not a one-time thing but a continual process.

In 2003, I was challenged to put feet to the plan that I had known for more than 30 years that God had for my life. When our son was about three years old, the Lord spoke to me that what He had for me would involve multicultural and interdenominational communities. I became aware of it literally when I began college in 1989. I had always been in a controlled environment at work and in my church community, but in the classroom, I was in the presence of many different cultures, with many different religions and many of those people had a great concept of and love for God. I had to let go of my stereotyping in order to be a productive student. As I began to let go, I could see God in many diverse ways. I had to let Him out of the box that I had unknowingly put Him in.

Following college, I worked in a mixed culture community for more than seven years. Again, I had to expand my way of thinking and the way I interacted with others, both naturally and spiritually. I was often aware of 1Corinthians 9:19-23. Especially the portions which read "...I made myself servant unto all, that I might gain the more...I am made all things to all men, that I might by all means save some...and this I do for the gospel's sake, that I might be partaker with you..."

It can be difficult to know when it is time to let go. Many times the signs are all there but because of loyalties and traditions we may not see them.

After 30 years as members of a church in Tacoma, my husband and I moved from Tacoma to Federal Way, Washington in 1995. When we moved, we now had to travel Highway 509 to church. After a time I noticed that I would get a headache by the time I was halfway to the bridge, (which was probably the halfway point to church.) I would be agitated at church and I would cry almost all the way back home.

I began to really investigate my feelings and my surroundings to get a clear picture as to the why of these things. I didn't like what I discovered. The headaches were because I was always unsure of how things would be when we got to the church. Would the meeting start on time? Would the ones who called the meeting or the ones in charge be there or would they call and say they were not coming? Would Jesus be the main attraction or protocol? After we ushered in and welcomed Jesus, would He be allowed to stay? I would be frustrated by the time I left and feel like it was *almost a waste of time*. However, with God's help, I've learned to keep the good and throw the rest away with the breath of kindness.

As I continue my walk with God, I can always feel a tugging in my heart to know more of who God is and how all of creation is connected with Him and to Him. But in order to know more, I have to continually allow new revelations to be imparted to me. The only way that will happen is when I unleash *my* pre-conceived thoughts (traditions) that are not Biblical based and scripturally sound. WHAT A PROCESS!!!!!

And this process *is not* an easy one. It was much easier for me to move into the natural realm with the multicultural components than it was for me in the spiritual, interdenominational part. After all, I had been who/what I was all of the 50 plus years of my life and I was a licensed Evangelist in a very conservative Pentecostal denomination.

As I began to walk out the spiritual process and to seek counsel from my spiritual covering, my words and actions were not interpreted as I had expected they would be. Therefore the guidance I so longed for from my mentor was not available. I had to lean solely on directions from God through the life of Abraham, Paul, the written Word and on the love and support of my husband. The Lord had warned me that it would not be easy to convince my mentor that building bridges to other denominations was what I was hearing God tell me to do.

With my husband's permission, I set myself apart for two days in my home before I spoke with anyone concerning what God was instructing me to do. It was a few days afterward before I took the next step and my life has not been the same since. I asked God to give me His standard by which I was to gauge the comments and attitudes that I would encounter. His answer was very clear to me: "the words that I speak are spirit and they are life" (John 6:63) "…the wisdom that is from above is first pure…" (James 3:17)

I have always been a loyal, faithful, stable and committed Christian. I was a member of the same congregation for more than 30 years. My life was not perfect but I never stopped pressing forward. My family and I encountered many struggles and hardships, but we always weathered the storms. I thought that the core of my heart was evident by my life and that my love for God and my family was obvious. I somehow expected those components to be relevant factors with my mentor in helping me process and chart the course in which God was instructing me. But the counsel I received was not in the direction in which I knew God was leading me.

I began to question my commitment. Was it to God? Was it to a tradition? A denomination? A family tree? Was it to what I thought was expected of me from man?

As I began to search my heart in the presence of God, I was scared straight with what I discovered. It's true that my love for God was genuine and my desire was to please Him in every way, if only it could be done with *no hassles*. During my devotion one day, I was shocked as the words from Psalm 45:10 leapt off the page at me: "Hearken o daughter and consider, incline thine ear; forget also thine own people and thy father's house." Earlier Galatians, Chapter1 had gotten my attention, where Paul spent time alone with God and knew that the revelation he was receiving was from God alone.

I asked my husband what he would think if he heard the words "hearken", "consider" and "incline thine ear" in one paragraph. His response was that someone was trying to get his attention and should be listened to. I had to really position myself to hear God because I needed clarity.

I recalled a time when I heard a prophet tell a pastor to get a new Bible because God wanted to give him new revelations. You know how we mark and highlight our Bibles as we read? God wanted to give him new insights. God reasoned within me that concept. I needed to seek God like a newborn babe desires the sincere milk of the Word. It was not for me to forget my foundation, but to release many of the manmade customs I had been taught. I needed to be entire and lacking nothing so that I would be prepared for what was to come.

I had been with a women's ministry in Florida for seven years and I knew that God wanted me to allow that connection to be a vehicle by which He would expand my ministry. However, I needed the freedom and approval from my church to seek out other faith-based denominations whose tenets were of the same Biblical foundation before I proceeded to establish relationships and build bridges. My husband understood this, so he would remain at our congregation until I felt the unction from God that *this is one*. Then Roy would accompany me on a visit. When I tried to explain this to my mentor and receive his blessing, everything changed.

God had told me to do as He had told Abraham, "get thee out of thy country and from thy kindred and from thy father's house unto a land that I will shew thee …and thou shalt be a blessing" (Genesis 12:1). My mentor and I never really got beyond this verse. After all, Abraham's family was pagan and my family was not. My mentor was a relative who had been mentored by my father. Family surrounded the church and the denomination where I attended. As my husband, mentor and I were talking one evening, my husband explained that it was a faith mission God was calling us to. I remembered God asking me once, "Loveth thou Me more than these?" from John 21:15. How could I choose between a God whom I have never seen and a people whom I've known all my life???

I began to walk out my God choice within the boundaries allowed by my mentor. But that was still not acceptable to him. I was expected to report my whereabouts at all times when I was not at my local church. I agreed to this. However, the following Sunday when Roy attempted to make contact with my mentor to advise him that I was at our home, he was unavailable. By the time my husband called him later that evening, the man of God was clearly irritated. As I tried to determine what his expectations were regarding my movements, things got increasingly worse.

Everything I did to preserve my relationship with this mentor was seemingly wrong. In hindsight, it may have offended him that I began to write letters to him rather than meeting face to face. I knew that I could be very direct and quick with my words, so in my attempts to be respectful, I wrote very cautiously. Each response that I received back from him was more heart wrenching. I was told to change my actions or surrender my credentials.

How does one make the choice between God and man? I saw no need to choose. We are all God's children, made from one blood and one in Christ. I only wanted to build bridges that would connect us with some of our other Christian families. Finally my husband stepped in and said "No more," I surrendered my credentials and we stopped attending that church.

Although I have moved into different geographical and religious settings, I still experience inner grief as I continue to release people from relationships formed during those 30 years that were endearing to me. It is important that I have no expectations, and that I continue to have unconditional love for them as God instructs me to. The pain is in the fact that it seems like they have no validation of the God within me outside of what that denomination tolerates. Although they admired and respected the anointing that was present in my life and the way I ministered, it seemed to all disappear when I left that church. It's as though I had left God.

It's sad to think that while many physical rules were overlooked—going to movies and wearing certain clothes—yet when the use of authority was given to disassociate with me, that was obeyed. It was painful and very offensive to me, especially when I'd been one of the most supportive persons in their lives.

However, I'm more aware than ever, that the battle is not between flesh and blood but against principalities and power, against the rulers of the darkness of this world, against spiritual wickedness in high places. And the enemy uses whoever and whatever opportunity he can to bring schisms and separations in the Body of Christ. I continue to let go of negative thoughts and feelings and trust God. All circumstances are bringing me to the expected end God has for me.

We need our foundational truths, our morals and family values, but it is important that we recognize when control, intimidation and manipulation are being used by those in authority to suppress people. We must learn to let go of being self-assertive in a negative way, learn how to say "no" without guilt, and learn when to say "yes" for the right reasons rather than out of a sense of obligation.

As we release and relinquish *our claim* on who we are, on the people who God allows to be in our lives, our ideologies and our expectations, we will realize that God is still in control. He is all of what we have been accustomed to and sooooooo much more. We must let go of all the pain of yesteryear and even yesterday. All of our past must be placed in God's control. Each day that we get up is "give us this day our daily bread." (Matthew 6:11) And each night as we lay down to rest, "I laid me down to sleep and my sleep was sweet." (Proverbs 3:24)

There is a poster that I bought for my mom in her last months of life said something like:

My name is **I AM**.
Living in the past is hard because My name is not *I was*.
Living in the future is hard because
My name is not *I will be*.
But living in this moment is not hard because *I am here*.
My name is **I AM**.

When the past is properly placed in our emotions, we can move forward with stronger weapons because our witness will be personal testimonies of *I know* and *I am persuaded*.

We will also be surprised to see that He already has our next assignment all lined up. Our coast has been enlarged, our insight expanded and we have been prepared to walk in new territory. All of the new territory is just another expression of who He is. For me, God already had an open door and He was just waiting for me to let Him out of the box and say yes to Him, again…and again…and again.

Sometimes the assignment may not be to do anything, go anyplace or be with any person. It may be a challenge to let go of our busyness and learn how to rest in Him and hear

His still small voice, to stand still and see the salvation of the Lord, and in so doing—grow.

I'm also becoming more aware of the letting go that we must do in regard to this earthly world and all it's possessions. When God is calling us home to be with Him, we need to be able to say goodbye to this world and it's pleasures and commend ourselves to God. We must learn to live in this world and enjoy its delights as a loose garment. This world is not our home; we are just pilgrims passing through.

Trust is the bridge we walk on as we let go. Our faith, hope and our expectation are not in anyone or anything that we feel or see, but our trust is in the all Mighty, all Powerful and all Knowing God. As we continue our walk, we will be able to say the words of Isaiah 12:2 with strong assurance: "Behold, God is my salvation; I will trust, and not be afraid: for the Lord Jehovah is my strength and my song; He also is become my salvation."

Listen*ing*

Early in life we learn to listen to many different voices. Some are voices of authority for instruction and insight while others are to influence us to partake of the negative. However, at some point we must learn to distinguish between them and hear the voice that is more important.

How do we know whether the voice that we hear is really the one we are supposed to listen to?

Is there a difference in hearing and listening? I believe there is.

To hear is to perceive sound or simply to have a sense of hearing. And to listen is to pay attention to; focus on; keep your mind on and adhere to. When I think of hearing, it is like the sound of baby talk—you hear the sounds but you have no idea of what is being said. Listening provides clarity and meaning to words. Many times before a person learns the art of listening, they began to formulate their response to a speaker as soon as they hear one point of interest. Then when they speak, they realize that what they thought they were responding to is inaccurate. When real listening takes place, the listener will repeat what they heard to make sure they are responding appropriately.

Listening involves paying close attention to not only the words, but the tone, expressions and body language of the speaker. It is a learned skill that involves reading between the lines and hearing the words not actually spoken. The heart as well as the ears must be involved in developing this skill. When we listen with our heart, we can respond with compassion rather than reacting from an emotional level. The other person's feelings are important no matter how direct and intense the response may be.

It is difficult to determine the real voice of authority when a person is unsure of who they are, has a lack of confidence in Whose they are or is unclear about the course of their destiny. But as the purpose for which God has designed them is understood, the voices that are ordained to help them reach their highest level of potential becomes clearer.

There will be many voices at different stages that can have great impact in shaping and molding our character. Many times we will learn who and *what not* to listen to before we learn who and *what to* listen to.

1Peter 1:10 tells us to give diligence to make our calling and election sure. As we confirm who we are in God, we will be better able to listen to the voices that will encourage, inspire and thrust us into the plan He has for us. If God has designed us to be leaders but we're always listening to followers, it will take us longer to reach our destiny, *if we ever reach it*. As we make our calling and election sure, negative voices that would deter us will be weeded out and we'll become more in tune to the voices that will help us to be all we're destined to be.

Listening is two-fold in the sense that sometimes it is for ourselves and at other times it is for someone else. Yet, there are times when it is for ourselves first and then for imparting to others as we share our testimonies.

Have you ever made a phone call, sent a thinking-of-you note or made an impromptu visit and were told *"that was just what I needed?"* That is listening and imparting to others.

I remember some years ago, my husband and I were impressed to take a care package to a single mom who was terminally ill. I felt very strange as I was selecting certain items to take, but the mystery was solved when we delivered the package. She and her children needed many of the items and had desired some of the others.

I was encouraged to be more in tune to my inner voice. Many times what seems minute to us is most important to someone else. God does supply our needs and many times He will give us our desires. And you and I may be the one whom God uses as the supplier to someone else.

We are the eyes, ears, arms and feet of Jesus. How can Jesus touch the world except through us, His ambassadors? We may be the only Jesus some will ever see. We never know if we are the planter, the waterer or if we are the one who will prepare the soil for planting. What is important is to do our all for His glory and bring increase to the family of God.

When we sense that God is ordering our steps, it could be dangerous to ask for the opinion of others or maybe even to mention it to others. They might challenge us so that we second guess or doubt what God spoke to us. Then our delivery of what God has given us may not be as effective.

God speaks to us according to the divine purpose He has for us. How can anyone else really understand us and many of our actions without knowing our destiny? We must listen intensely and pray for godly revelation because we will be held accountable for what God speaks to us and our obedience to it. We may need to do as Paul did in Galatians 1:15,16, confer with no man and commune, for a time only with God, our Maker.

We must use the Word of God as our guide when we are asking for the opinion of others. Jesus said in John 6:63 that the words He speaks are spirit and life. In the book of James it's said, "The wisdom that is from above is first pure, peaceable, gentle, easy to be entreated, full of mercy and good fruits, without partiality and without hypocrisy." (James 3:17).

I have a mental picture of a mom disciplining a child with the child holding on to the mom's skirt and crying at the same time. This is the way I imagine God expects us to respond when He is speaking to us. Especially when it is painful and we don't understand. Yes, His words and directions are sometimes stern, direct and painful, but we cling to Him because His firmness is also a part of His love and compassion.

This is a powerful tool in helping me to get my children to listen to me. Especially in delicate matters when there are Biblical principles to adhere to. I want to be sure that my word does not deter them from listening to the voice of God. This also helps me when I hear sermons and *words from God* through humankind. If my spirit becomes irritated to borderline angry and I want to run and not look back, I question the motive and the intent of the messenger. After a while, when my spirit is calm and I pray that if there is a message from God I will hear it and listen for His direction.

I have truly learned to listen to my inner man when hearing from others because even when there are disagreements, they can be shared agreeably. When I was in a major transition of life and of the many people I wanted to run from, I'm thankful for a brother who said to me, in a questioning but calm manner, "just be careful and prayerful." He even displayed to me the heart of a shepherd, (leaving the 99 to find the one) when he took a detour of more than 200 miles to come and see about me. That kept my heart open to not only hear him, but to listen to him.

There was a time when I was impressed to share a tape with someone who was fighting cancer and did not profess to have a relationship/fellowship with God. When I shared this thought with someone else, it was suggested that that might not be a good idea because of the strong content. I hesitated to send it and the more I procrastinated, the more my spirit became restless. I attuned my ear to listen again to the voice within and knew what I should do regardless of how it might be received. Sometime later, at a victory celebration, the comment was made that what I had sent was "one of the most precious encouragements we had received."

In September 2002, while visiting our oldest daughter in Colorado Springs, I experienced a time of listening that I will not forget. My husband, Roy, was outside on her patio up on a ladder cleaning the gutters of her house when she and I decided to go shopping. She went upstairs and I went downstairs to get ready to go. Nearly simultaneously, we met each other on the main floor. Both of us felt we couldn't leave with Roy outside on the ladder. As we went outside to tell him to either get off the ladder until we returned or else go with us, we discovered he had fallen off the ladder onto a cement floor. He could not move nor could he call for help. But because my daughter and I had both been listening to that inner voice within us, we found him in a matter of seconds and were able to call for help.

God uses many different things and situations to get us to listen—distraught relationships with family, friends and co-workers, employment or financial situations, failing health, and sometimes even death. We can listen with our feelings, our eyes, our inner premonition, or intuition (some call it a sixth sense). To Christians it is commonly known as an unction from the Holy Spirit.

Listening is a never-ending development. We can hear the same thing time and time again, and each time we hear it, it has a different impact on our life. Life is composed of many different seasons. As we grow, our abilities progress from merely hearing to listening more profoundly. The same words we heard yesterday have a completely different meaning today because the season has changed.

God's Word and wisdom are eternal; we must keep our hearts in tune.
LISTEN…

Listen…

listen.

Help Me Say Goodbye

To say goodbye on an ordinary day under normal circumstances seems to be no big deal, but when you feel that it may be your last time to see that person, saying goodbye has a completely different meaning. More so than meaning, a whole different feeling. And when you're trying to help a terminal patient say goodbye to this world with its pleasures, friends and family, it is different even yet.

I don't think I noticed the difference in these components between life and death until my Mother was in her final months of life on earth in 1998.

Whereas my oldest sister and my first grandchild were deceased some years ago, it was quite different with Mama.

I had thought one year before Mama passed that she was in her final months and for reasons unknown, she was in a struggle.

After a major episode of illness I became really concerned about her demeanor and began to watch closely and pray carefully. During this time I had a dream that involved my father and one of the missionaries from our church, which was quite disturbing. Missionary White came into the room where I was packing my mom's suitcase and told me to hurry because my father was outside waiting for her. I was truly alarmed by this dream because both my father and Missionary White were deceased.

At this time also, the Book Club I was in was reading the book, *Pilgrim's Progress*. I was in the last chapter when the pilgrim was crossing the river and became a bit fearful. As I read those pages it seemed as though God was speaking to me and instructing me to help usher Mama over to the other side.

My thought process began to change. I began to think of why we live the way we do, as Christians. Our daily walk, our ethics, our morals…we live the way we do because we desire to see Jesus, hear Him say "Well done" and live with Him eternally. Some will be raptured and others who have died will meet Him in the clouds. But we must leave this earth in order to be with Him.

Jesus told us in John 14 that He was going to His Father to prepare a place for us where there were many mansions and that He was coming again to receive us unto Himself. In the Book of Revelation, Heaven is described as a physical place with walls of jasper, gates of pearl and streets of pure gold.

When I began to think of Jesus preparing a place for us and the description in Revelation, it became easier for me to talk with my mom about being in Heaven, a prepared placed with Jesus and God versus being here on earth suffering.

God had blessed us to enjoy life with her for 88 years and they had been good years. I could not bear to see her suffer nor was it easy to see her lose the use of her motor skills. She was being reduced to a baby-like stage where we had to bathe her and change her like a baby. It wasn't good for her morale. Neither do I believe that God intends for us, His saints, to lose our dignity before we leave this earth.

When I would go and visit with her, I would talk about being a prepared vessel to be with Jesus in that prepared place. I would tell her to imagine it—the peace, the beauty and the rest from this world's weariness.

When the time came to say goodbye, it really was an awesome moment.

Two of my older siblings and I were in the room with her when she took her last breath. My oldest sister, who is an evangelist, laid the Bible on the bed beside Mama and opened it to Revelation, chapter 21. As Alice began to read, the whole atmosphere in the room began to change. The glory of God truly filled the room with brightness and a peace that is indescribable. Mama opened her eyes, lifted her hands and gave a clap of praise that was so like her, turned her head, closed her eyes again and went on to Heaven. The presence of the Lord was so overwhelming that we were rejoicing and weeping at the same time.

Since that day, my attitude toward the death of a saint has really taken on a new meaning. I find it difficult to prolong one's life when all the signs of death are present. When there is *struggle*, I begin to pray that God will give direction and clarity as to what could be the hindrance, how to handle the obstruction and how to help in the process of saying goodbye to a dying world and how to say, as Jesus did, "Father, into Thy hands I commend my spirit."

There have been several goodbyes since Mama. I'm thankful for the experience I had in her home-going because it has helped me to help others in what is one of the most difficult and dreadful times that one must go through.

We must leave the land of the dying to enter the
land of the living by saying...
Goodbye.

When we say goodbye, it is not final. In many cases,
we are really saying,
"See you later!"

Give Love Away

Have you ever looked at life's situations and perplexities and thought, "If only I could help or make a difference?"

I was reading in a *Chicken Soup for the Soul* book about a judge who was known as the "Hugging Judge." The bumper sticker on his car read, "Don't bug me, hug me." The story cited more incidents where lives had been touched by his hugging than by his judging.

I thought of these words to a song: "If I can cheer somebody with a word of a song, then my living shall not be in vain."

I have been known for giving on-time hugs. That story challenged me to be even more of an active giver of the love Christ has shown to me. I cannot change the world system, keep the stock market from crashing, cure cancer or make everyone happy, but I can brighten the corner where I am.

In this microwave age of quick fixes and do your own thing, I can have a patient, pleasant tone in my voice as I communicate with friends and family (even when I'm frustrated) and on the telephone. I can have pleasant, light conversation with the people around me at the checkout stand. I can take the time to smile at the driver in the car beside me at the stop light. I can try and live so that my personality is user-friendly so that people will not be intimated, feel harassed or want to leave when they see me coming! I once heard a preacher say that he witnesses all the time and every once in a while he opens his mouth and says something.

> *God so loved the world that*
> *He gave His only begotten son.*
> *Christ loved the church and gave Himself for it.*

Understanding the real meaning of love will help us give it away.

When I think of love, I think of feelings and actions that are shared. When love is given away, it is shared with others with the expectation of nothing in return. What comes from the heart reaches the heart. When the love of God is in our hearts, it does not matter what one's circumstance may be—their heart is still open to the Spirit of God to receive prompts to minister to others.

I recall a time when I was in the midst of my most life-changing traumatic experience that I had a dream about one of my church sisters. I was dealing with my teenage daughter's unwed-pregnancy and the death of this first grandchild along with my husbands' near death accident. Yet my spirit was still open to give love. In the dream Ruth was in great difficult pain. When I awoke I was in great pain. My hand was on the lower part of my stomach and I was praying in the Spirit. I didn't know what it was, but I knew that whatever it was, she would be okay. When I shared the dream with her, she expressed joy and began to share with me her situation.

Ruth showed me a picture of an ultra-sound which revealed that she was pregnant but that with this pregnancy there was also a tumor. Would she have the tumor removed, abort the baby or chose neither? She chose to do neither. She continued with her pregnancy and allowed the tumor to remain. In spite of the challenges she faced during her pregnancy, she gave birth to a healthy, bouncy baby boy. If I recall correctly, she did not have surgery following that birth and within a two year span she gave birth to another healthy son. These two sons are now in college.

As I think of this now, I'm blessed to know that in my heart of hearts, it is like Jesus. He is our Perfect Example. As He was dying on the cross He was our Intercessor. He asked His Father to forgive those who were crucifying Him. He took the time to give salvation and comfort to the thief who was on the cross beside Him. I'm truly thankful that He honored and comforted the women who were in the great crowd following after Him to the place of crucifixion. He used a term of endearment, Daughters of Jerusalem, weep not for me (Luke 23:28).

Oftentimes we think that to give love is to give gifts that have been bought with money, but there are many ways to give love away without the cost of a penny. There are times when a listening ear is welcome, especially when it is without judgment or criticism. A shoulder to cry on, an act of kindness and service are also gifts of godly love.

My husband volunteers with a community outreach in our town and at times he leaves food baskets and flowers at the homes of family and friends. The needs that are met and the spirits that are lifted are God's way of adding hope to the lives of others. He has also, on occasion, taken food to the streets and randomly given to the homeless. What a way to give love!

A favorite scripture text of mine is Proverbs 11:25, "the liberal soul shall be made fat: and he that watereth shall be watered also himself."

Often when I am in a low, out-of-sorts mood, I reach out beyond myself by sending cards and making phone calls to shut-ins, the elderly, young wives and mothers and whomever the Lord will lay on my heart. I try and follow the rule of "...as ye would that men should do to you, do ye also to them likewise" (Luke 6:31), and by the time I have finished with a few cards and a call or two, my spirit is lifted and I've received what I've given away—the love and presence of a loving God.

When we pray with supplications and intercession in the Spirit, we are giving love away. When the Spirit prays, we reach and touch needs that may not have been spoken in words and lives are changed. As we allow our spirit to be open to the Spirit of God, even when we least expect it, through dreams and visions, we give love away.

Some people give, give and give. They share their talents, their time, their resources and their money, but it is not with love. It is to be seen, for recognition, for status, for control. But when true love is given away, it is given with the motive and attitude of our Heavenly Father, unconditionally.

While visiting in St. Louis, Missouri one church announcer began her announcements with this attention getter:

Smiling is infectious; you catch it like the flu.
When someone smiled at me today, I started smiling too.
I passed around the corner and people saw my grin.
When they smiled back,
I realized I'd passed it on to them!
I thought about that grin and realized its worth.
A single smile just like mine
could travel `round the earth.
So, if you feel a smile begin...
don't leave it undetected.
Start an epidemic quick, and get the world infected!
What a simple thing to do—to give love away.
Let's continue it today!

S M I L E!

Hurry Up and Wait

Are you one of those people who's always running late or just making the deadline for whatever the situation? I am.

This time I determined that I would be at the airport an hour before my departure time (this was before 9/11) only to find out that the plane was delayed for two hours. At first I was very agitated. My flight was only 35 minutes long and it was just a four hour drive to my destination and there I sat. For what? To hurry up and wait!

After a moment, I began to focus on the why. Since I believe that all things work together for good and nothing happens unless God allows it, I began to look for reasons— maybe a hijack…maybe I got there early because of an accident later on the freeway…maybe to avoid a landing accident…maybe…maybe…maybe. Since I had no answers, I decided that I would pull out my pen and pad to write.

I was amazed at how I began to observe and evaluate my surroundings. I saw two young people who had spiked haircuts with very bright colors traveling with musical instruments. I could feel that I wanted to believe that they were of the "punk rock" generation with no regard for normality. Yet I sensed an unction to sit beside them. I did. After sensing no negative vibes, I initiated casual chit chat. What a revelation!!! They were on their way back to college, their mom was accompanying them and they were to meet with another brother at their destination. They were polite, respectful and had a good sense of purpose.

I thought of how unfair it was of me to assume negative thoughts before we interacted. And how often we have negative assumptions because of how "they look" and how we stereotype.

As we talked, I thought of one of my daughters who is "very different," as we church society say. I thought of how I've said, "If only they could look beyond her hair color, hair style, tattoos and body piercings, they would know that she is a good person with a tender heart," and yet, I was doing the same thing...assuming, judging, stereotyping!!!

My attitude began to change and I became even more aware of my surroundings in search of what God was intending for me to see. I put aside my pre-conceived judgmental attitude and put on a soft approachable demeanor. I don't know if anyone around me noticed a change in my manner, but I did.

I glanced across the aisle and saw an older male with tattoos all on his arm. Again, I thought of my daughter. I said a prayer for her that God would reveal Himself to her in a very real way and use all of who she is and the things that HE has allowed her to encounter to be a witness for Him at His appropriate time and to help me love her openly and unconditionally. I also said a prayer for those who were sitting close around me and thanked God that He had used them to help me wait in His presence and grow. I began to realize the bonuses I had received by waiting.

Across from me sat an older woman who made me think of my mom who had gone to be with the Lord in May 1998. This lady had such a quiet, reserved dignity about her that I was reminded that we should always, in all circumstances, cause those around us to sense a peace within us that surpasses understanding. She was the essence of a "lady." I thought of how blessed I was to have had *such a lady* as my mom and how grateful I was of the many hours we had spent together. Because my siblings and I are spread from Washington state to Arkansas to Washington, D.C., I also thanked God and appreciated Him for taking care of Mama as she traveled from state to state and city to city to visit with us.

I thought of when Mama traveled, how she always had some sort of handcraft to do. I'm confident that the majority of her seven children, 38 grandchildren and 100-plus great-grandchildren have items in their homes that were made by her. Not to mention the recipes and her godly, yet witty character. She left such a legacy.

As I was sitting, I also noticed a woman who was very agitated because of the delayed flight. I prayed for her silently and asked the Lord if I were to be an instrument for Him to her.

While on my way to use my lunch voucher (another bonus), the agitated lady and I made eye contact in passing and I took the opportunity to smile and speak. Her response was friendly and I took a chance to make conversation. I mentioned that I had noticed her agitation earlier and asked if she was feeling better. She shared with me why she had been so irritated and as we talked, I told her of my feelings and how I had gone through the *maybes* and the *what ifs* in my mind and my conclusions. What an opportunity to share God. She thanked me for taking the time to notice and to care about her. She felt better.

Yes, I'm still improving on my arrival times, and when I have to wait, I've learned how to be more patient and know that God is allowing the delay and if I trust Him, everything will be okay.

Delayed gratification is a lost art. We live in a microwave society. We want it now or at least within the next fifteen minutes. Have you noticed that when food is warmed in the microwave, it doesn't retain its heat long? But when it is heated on the stove or in the oven, the heat is thorough, complete, from the inside out with lasting warmth.

Waiting is time consuming and often it does seem useless, however; the benefits can be rewarding.

It is in waiting, or shall I say in patient waiting, that God can reveal to us what He has for us and what we need to do to receive it. Patience is a good character builder and an important component to Christian growth. As we develop it, we will also be aware of temperance, experience, godliness and kindness built upon love. When these elements are present, we are neither barren nor unfruitful in the knowledge of our Lord and our witness is stronger.

I've also learned to carry reading material and puzzle books along with pen and paper. They help the time go by faster and lessen the tension and stress on me and whoever my companion maybe.

So now as I travel from state to state, from city to city, by car or plane, and even when I go from home to work, to church or to play; when I have to wait for a traveling companion, the traffic or the traffic controller, (and yes, even when I'm late because of me), I'm still human and have my inner debates, but Lord, I ask You to grant me more patience as I hurry up to wait.

"But let patience have her perfect work, that ye may be perfect and entire, wanting nothing." James 1:4

In God Alone

In a crowded room, but alone.
A member of a large close-knit family, but alone.
A member of a large Christian community,
on several ministry boards, yet alone.
A spouse, children, friends and associates,
but still an emptiness.
In the heart that yearns to be listened to,
understood and nurtured…
What is one to do?

For the umpteenth time, I hear a quiet voice saying, "I'm here" and as I begin to quiet my spirit and gather my emotions, I begin to sense stillness in the air.

When I retire for the night, I set my television timer on the Daystar channel and allow the sound of soft music to continue to soothe my aching soul. One evening, as the aches began to diminish, I looked at the screen and I read these words, "My soul finds peace in God alone." I felt a quickening in my spirit and began to rest in His presence.

The more my spirit rested, the more I felt a release in my flesh. David said in Psalm 16:9b, "my flesh also shall rest in hope."

The more I relaxed, the more I knew He was there.

Other scripture texts scrolled across the screen and each time I looked up, they were focused on "God alone."

Can I say like Isaiah did in Isaiah 30:15b: "…in returning and rest shall ye be saved; in quietness and in confidence shall be your strength?"

I think I can!
I now have the security of being alone, but not lonely.
The assurance that He will never leave me nor forsake me.
I know that being alone, but in His presence,
is where I belong.
I am made in His image, designed for a specific purpose,
and no one can orchestrate me for that purpose but Him.
So away from the possibility of generational failures;
the stagnation of Christian denominational
traditions and rituals;
the popular opinions of friends and associates;
I come...
I linger...
I abide…
in the garden… alone
where He molds me to be all He designed me to be
when He first thought of me.

**For God alone my soul waits in silence; from
Him comes my salvation.**
Psalm 62:1 (AMP)

I Just Wanna Be Me

At what age must I be before I feel free?
Free to say what I feel without being condemned?
Free to look like who I am without being damned?
Free to "not be" who you think I should be
and not be called rebellious?
When do you look at me and see "me"
and not the visions of who you wish I were?
When do you judge me by my character
and not by the blood in my veins?
There is a part of God in me that screams to be set free.

I yearn for unconditional love that will validate and mentor the innate qualities God has placed within me; to develop these qualities to their highest level of potential so that they may be used for the edification of the ministry and for God's glory.

As I become convinced that God is my all and all and allow Him to be my satisfying portion, I will choose to not sit here and die, but I will shake the dust from my feet, wipe my weary eyes and run…I no longer ask you to like me, just respect the creation God has made me to be and release me.

Release me from being the brunt of your unresolved anger.
Release me from being the stronghold
of your denied jealousy.
Release me from being the conversation
of your seeds of discord.
Release me and set me free.

However, in case you don't release me, I have decided to release myself. I will dwell in my secret closet under my Creator's shadow...

where there is acceptance,
where there is peace,
where there is shelter from the storm
and more than anything,
where there is unconditional love.

In God's love I find the security that allows me the privilege of failing while I try. I find gentle correction when I err, firm affirmation when I've done well and strong courage to try and try again. I find the confidence to be a quiet presence. Because even when I am quiet, He speaks through me, for His glory is a shield about me and He is the lifter of my head.

I just wanna be me!!!

I just wanna be all who God has designed me to be when He first thought of me. Even when I am in the furnace of affliction and in the refiner's fire, I will praise, worship and honor my God—for when I am tried I shall come forth as pure gold. As I press forward, I find the inner strength that I have heard about and read about for years and I see it become a reality in my life and I like it.

I like being an exhorter, I like being a worshiper, I like being a teacher. I like being used of God as His servant. I like knowing that God gave me a rich family heritage from where I get my stamina, my zeal. I love loving God. I love worshipping Him, I love serving Him. I love being in Him for it is *in Him* I live, I move and I have my being.

I was in my late forties when I was told of some circumstances surrounding my conception and birth. My father, Papa, as we called him, was very ill and not expected to live. When a pastor traveling through our hometown felt an unction by God to stop for a visit. He found Papa gravely ill. This pastor gathered my father into his arms and walked the floor with him until the Lord breathed into him again the freshness of life. It was after this that I was conceived. I'm told that I was very small and thus my father called me "Lil' Bit."

This was an important time in Papa's life! Can you imagine the excitement of resurrection!!!! Not only had he been given another chance to live, he was given the strength and energy to be sexually active and produce another child. Wow — what a celebration, at least for my father. (Now, my mom's feeling is a whole 'nother story.)

Papa was in his forties and Mama was in her late thirties, plus I was child number eleven. From the time I heard this story, my attitude toward me changed. That's why:

I've gotta be "ME."
For I am fearfully and wonderfully made;
I am a powerful possibility,
I am a great big ball of potentiality;
And I love life.

The words of David from Psalm 139:14-17 (AMP/KJV) have a new meaning to me. Wonderful are Your works, and that my inner self knows right well. My frame (my substance) was not hidden from You when I was being intricately and curiously wrought. Thine eyes saw my substance, yet being unperfect; and in thy book all my members were written, which in continuance were fashioned, when as yet there was none of them. How precious also are thy thoughts unto me, O God! How great is the sum of them!

Yes, I am "ME."
I am made in His image, created in His likeness;
I am a Designer's original,
made for a divine purpose, for such a time as this.

I'm so thankful to all who helped me find "me." Of the many things I appreciate about my professors at Evergreen College, the important one is that as they observed me and instructed me as a student. They helped to define the person within. They never criticized or spoke negatively of anything or anyone in my life. They just helped me to personalize me and to construct ways in which I could be me in the midst of whatever situation I encountered.

The theme of our first quarter was Critical Thinking, and boy was that a challenge!!! I was forced to identify and confront my code of ethics and the why of them. I began to recognize the me whom others dictated that I be, and I did not like it. It was not ushering me into who I felt God wanted me to be. But I did not give up and often, I did not give in.

By the end of my first year, one of my instructors named me as a pastoral consultant to anyone who needed personal counseling while attending school. That made me more determined than ever to wanna be me.

After graduating from Evergreen College, I enrolled in IBET, a Christian college, where I took Christian Counseling. I needed to be more aware of the me inside of me and how to personify me in truth, without denying the God in me or my love for life. It was also important that I be as inoffensive as possible. The real reason for much of my schooling was not to teach others, but to help me personalize "me."

I can see clearly now, the fog has lifted;
I can see obstacles that are placed in my path;
I'm aware of the darkness that's designed
to make me stumble;
but with God I know,
there's gonna be bright sunshiny days.
I choose to develop the gift of life that God gave to me
And give it back as my gift to Him,
by being "ME".

Taking *It* Back

"And from the days of John the Baptist until now
the kingdom of heaven suffereth violence, and the
violent take it by force." (Matthew 11:12)

"Ye are of God, little children, and have overcome them:
because greater is He that is in you, than he that is
in the world." (I John 4:4)

There comes a time in life when we must wake up and smell the coffee. We must realize that the enemy is out to destroy us and everything that our hands touch, especially our human relationships. It is human relationships that display the love of God. For when we have unconditional love one *to* another, God is seen. Families make up church congregations and the church and families are two components that are designed to represent the heart of God.

I discovered some time ago that the war is not amongst humankind, but between God and satan. We humans are caught in the middle. However, when we make God our choice and allow Him to be our Savior and Lord, He is our mediator and we are no longer in the middle. Yet it takes us a while to comprehend the fact that we are more than conquerors through Christ Jesus, our Lord, and the battle is not ours but His.

The song that says, "I went to the enemy's camp and I took back what he stole from me," is often on my mind. I recall in April, 1999 when I went to a Women's Fellowship Breakfast in Seattle, Washington and through words of exhortation to me, I was reminded that I am not afraid of the enemy, that I had gone into his camp and taken back my children and that the enemy fears the God in my life when he sees me coming.

At the time, two of our four children were not saved and although I saw no immediate change, my faith was strengthened and I held firm to my faith. I also dare to say that things got worse before they got better.

My oldest daughter, who was married to a military man and an ordained preacher, divorced after 13 years. My son presented me with a grandson out-of-wedlock four days after we buried my mom and my youngest daughter, who had been married for three years, was no longer interested in even trying to make it work. All of this was in addition to the fact that my husband is on total disability because of an industrial accident that left him almost dead. Although he is able to be active, he is limited and in pain 99.9% of the time. That is not always good, mentally or emotionally, for the morale of a man's man, if you know what I mean. And who gets the short end of the stick when the temperament is a bit testy and bears much of the pain?!?!?.. You guessed it—me, the spouse.

After being somewhat handicapped myself for months, with shingles and a broken hand, I had to put myself in remembrance of Whose I am and tell the devil that he is not the boss of me. My resolve was like Job: "For though He slay *me, yet will I trust in him."* (Job 13:15)

I *am* victorious because I am going forward *in spite* of what I see or how I feel. My confidence is in knowing that God is my refuge and my strong tower. I decided that as long as I have any being I will allow God to be Lord of my life. He knows my end and He is the Author and Finisher of my faith. It is in Him I live, move and have my being. Each day that He allows me to see, He will provide me with the strength that I need to glorify Him. I *choose* every day to acknowledge Him and let Him order my steps.

Sometimes it may seem like I am sitting down or standing still, and outwardly that may be true, but inwardly, I am standing tall and I am strong. In my heart, my mind and my spirit, I know that no matter what the enemy puts in my way to try and stop me, I will never say fail. In the Word of God I have a hiding place. The Bible is true and His promises to me are sure. Even if I don't see all things fulfilled while on earth, I know that I have a home eternally in heaven and all of His promises will be fulfilled.

"It" presents itself in many forms—some are within and some are without. The *its* that are within are usually the ones that do the most damage, those mind badgers. They attack our self-esteem, self-awareness and our self-worth. These components manifest themselves in outward behaviors that affect our body and our relationships which also have a great impact on our Christian journey.

The things we encounter in society can make us more susceptible to desire the opinions and praise of others. We can become vulnerable to comparing ourselves with each other more than we focus and maintain our reaching forth unto the things that are of the High calling.

We must be watchful and aware of the wiles of the enemy, identify what he is trying to steal, kill and destroy and with the authority that Christ has given us, continue to push forward.

Our pastor recently finished a series on Recovering Our Lives. One of his base scriptures has made me more determined to *take it all back*. That text is 1 Samuel 30:18,19, "And David recovered **all**...and there was nothing lacking to them, neither small nor great, neither sons nor daughters, neither spoil, nor any thing that they had taken...David recovered **all**."

During the early months after my husband's accident, the Lord would often comfort me with the following scriptures:

- Joel 2: 25, "And I will restore to you the years that the locust hath eaten..."
- Psalm 91:15,16, "He shall call upon me, and I will answer him: I will be with him in trouble; I will deliver him, and honour him. With long life will I satisfy him and shew him my salvation."
- John 16:33, "These things I have spoken unto you, that in me ye might have peace. In the world ye shall have tribulation: but be of good cheer; I have overcome the world."

There are times when I feel like the "its" have me, but I am committed to loving God with all my heart, my mind, my soul and my strength. And when I am weak, He is strong. I've learned to surround myself with positive influences that speak to the inner me. These influences are the people who I associate and fellowship with, the things I do and the places I go.

It's easier to take *it* back when we know where it was lost. I lost my *it* in becoming a people pleaser, trying to fit in. I soon found out that I didn't fit in, but instead of letting go and finding new relations, I continued to give and discovered that enough is never enough and good is never good enough.

After three bad falls and three surgeries on my left hand, a dear friend made the comment, "When you pay closer attention to what God is saying to you, you may quit falling." Guess what? She was correct.

After I fell down some stairs in my home in June of 2003, in a store in August of 2003 and had the third surgery in

September of that same year, I thought she might be correct. I decided to do self-inventory again.

As I went over many of the things God had shared with me along life's way, I decided that this time I would do things as I felt God was saying to me, regardless. I remember distinctly hearing God speak to me saying, "no partial obedience." At first I didn't understand. But the more I began to rehearse words of knowledge and scripture verses, the clearer it became.

Isaiah 58 has always been one of my prophetic chapters and during this time verses 8 and 10b spoke to my heart: "Then shall thy light break forth as the morning, and thine health shall spring forth speedily; and thy righteousness shall go before thee; the glory of the Lord shall be thy rereward...then shall thy light rise in obscurity, and thy darkness be as the noon day."

The human part of us always wants to know the details before we just let go and free fall. We want to know what direction, how far, how long, etc. But as I began to walk out my letting go, *then* the way became clearer. I'm now really beginning to understand "...we walk by faith, not by sight." (2 Corinthians 5:7)

God has not changed His format. When we choose to obey Him and to trust Him, He gives us our bread, our direction, and our assignments day by day.

Yes, I took my children back from the enemy and now my husband, our four children and I are standing tall and fighting the enemy together. On Christ, the Solid Rock I (we) will continue to stand. I will recover self-worth, self-confidence, finances, favor, relationships and health. More than anything, I will recover my rightful place in this Christian army.

"We are troubled on every side, yet not distressed; we are perplexed, but not in despair; persecuted, but not forsaken; cast down, but not destroyed."
2 Corinthians 4:8,9

"Again, I say unto you, that if (*when*) two of you shall agree on earth as touching any thing that they shall ask, it shall be done for them of my Father which is in heaven. For where two or three are gathered together in my name, there am I in the midst of them."
Matthew 18:19, 20

When two pray, prison doors can be opened
and bands can be loosed.
Acts 16:25, 26

Pray on, my child!!!

Transitions

One thing I have found to be consistent in life is change. I once read a poster that stated, "By the time I get both ends to meet, someone moves one of the ends." We must develop agility in our persona like that of the palm tree. Agility will help us to be alert and give us the ability to act or react with a quickness and nimbleness to go with the flow. Or we will always be in broken pieces.

Even when it doesn't make sense, we must understand that we will never understand God's ways. His ways and His thoughts are not like ours, but when we allow the Creator to be present in all things...

> The bitter can be sweet
> The little can be enough
> And peace can be in the midst of the storm.

Transitions continue from birth to death. Some are God ordained, some are setups from satan and others occur because of personal choices. But let us remember that no matter how they come, God is the final authority in allowing them to happen. They are God's way of moving us to the place of destiny that He has designed for us. They are the passage from one place to another. Although the passage, the route by which we pass through or travel, may change with each transition, we can be assured that each one is a push of preparation for our eternal purpose.

When we view transitions simply as a change, we will not panic. God, in creation, instituted change—day/night, land/water, earth/firmament, the four seasons, the stages from infancy to adulthood, etc. Yet, change is a bit scary. Change may bring opposition; opposition can bring opportunity; opportunity brings a chance to grow and growth is a process.

During the growth process it is important that we keep our focus on the *main thing,* for there will be many distractions. I have made it a rule of thumb to not make any major decisions that are not associated with the change. However, I do try and determine:

1. What is the cause of this change?
2. The need?
3. Is it long term or short term?
4. How will it affect my life?
5. My husband's life?
6. My extended family?
7. Will it have an impact on the Body of Christ?

It is important to NOT neglect or let go of our personal relationship with our Lord Jesus Christ and Christian fellowship. Because these times gives us the opportunity to revaluate our relationships, our priorities and our values; to look down the line and see if and how far we have strayed from the plum line or standard.

I was born and raised in the South and we changed our wardrobe according to the season. We should keep in mind that all things and all people and all relationships may not be consistent in all transitions of our lives. Although people may be in our life our entire life, the relationship may be more intimate at different seasons and for different reasons.

Because change is inevitable, it is to our benefit when we don't resist it. When we are open and flexible to the transition, according to the principles and standards of holiness, the challenge will be one of growth and not to our detriment.

Godly principles must never be compromised. But it is possible, depending on the place and the kind of change being encountered, that there might need to be some alterations in our approach and application. Even when the transition doesn't end the way we expect it to, our experience can be a profitable testimony to share as our territory is enlarged.

Remember this…

With God, *there are no failures—only results and* **outcomes.** *(author unknown).*

Why Not You?

Iremember very well the day I was standing over my husband, looking down on his swollen head, with one eye gone and the threat of losing the other, asking God, "Why?" In the midst of silent tears streaming down my face, I could hear Him quietly say to me, "Why not you?"

At the time, I had no understanding of that response, but as I positioned myself before God, He assured me that He had allowed these happenings and if I trusted Him, He would be my guiding light.

It is true; things do come to make us strong. And when we choose to lean into the situation instead of fighting against it, our experience will give us an opportunity to have a more intimate relationship with the "I AM."

When relationship with the I AM is in constant fellowship, even when I'm at my wit's end and it seems like the forces of hell have been let loosed on me, I can stand. I know that as I look to Jesus, His light will shine on me and my life will be a mirror that reflects Him.

I now quote the entire verse of 2 Corinthians 12:9, "And He said unto me, My grace is sufficient for thee: for my strength is made perfect in weakness. Most gladly therefore will I rather glory in my infirmities, that the power of Christ may rest upon me." The latter portion takes the pressure off of me and it allows me to be human. For in admitting my weaknesses, God is glorified.

It is me because I was chosen before the foundation of the world, before I was shaped in my mother's womb, to be a pen for the handwriting of God to bring glory and honor to Him. I am one of His epistles, known and read among men, a light which cannot be hid.

My sister, it is you because God chose womanhood as the birth canal to bring forth new life. If you feel like your life is all out of sorts and there is no hope or if you're saying to yourself, "How can this possibly be?" think of Mary, the mother of Jesus. The Bible reports Mary's response to the changes God was implementing in her life. When the angel told Mary that "the Holy Ghost shall come upon thee, and the power of the Highest shall overshadow thee..." Even though she was troubled at the angel's saying, her response was "...be it unto me according to thy word." (Luke 1:35, 38) That greatly impressed me!

We must know that giving birth is no easy chore; it takes blood, sweat and tears. Oh, did I say blood, sweat and tears? And may I add, time, patience and endurance. Women bring newness to many arenas in life. Can you imagine what the world would be like without our creativity, our passion and our intuitiveness? In my mind I can hear some of you thinking, "It would be less chaotic, a bit more peaceful." Yeah, but it would also be a bit boring, don't you think? But don't fret, my sister, because believe it or not, whatever you are facing, God has called you highly favored and blessed.

My brother, it is you because God ordained you as the head. You are the one to who, God gave dominion and to have the last say-so concerning decisions—whether you have a family of not. When you don't feel like it, and you don't wanna feel like it, you are to be (especially to your family) as Christ is to the church and give yourself as a servant. When you have that strong desire for greatness, remember, he that is greatest among you shall be servant of all. Now don't take these words as an excuse to not ascribe to be all God intends for you to be. Just know that God never expects anything from anyone without providing instructions.

And further study as to how Christ was able to submit Himself as a Servant, will show that He knew His purpose. When the going got tough, He got going. He spent quality time with his Father God, and to His Father He commended His will. And just as the church loves, honors and respects His sovereignty, you too, will receive your just due from those in your life. Some are chosen in the furnace of affliction; some must go through the fire; some go through the floods, but we all must go through the blood.

Sometimes we think we are in charge, but we're not. We have been bought with a price, we are not our own and the price tag requires us to be available for Kingdom work at all times. When I mentioned this to one of my goddaughters, her question was, "Does the price ever get marked down?" At the time I said "No," but as I thought about it, the Lord said "Yes." I asked, "How?" He said, "With the pride of life, the lust of the flesh and the lust of the eye." (I John 2:16) "How do we do that, Lord," I asked?

God explained that when we go through our life's experiences and get hurt, disappointed, angry, battered and bruised, we build walls and barriers. These walls and barriers cause us to wear masks and disguises so that we do not share our pain, or our weakness. We "mark down" the price that Christ paid for us by pretending like we have it all together instead of allowing our pain to be turned into ministry and bring glory to God. We are to show forth the praises of Him who hath called us and not to ourselves.

We must know that God doesn't put more on us than we can bear, and every negative that we experience can be a positive influence in someone else's situation. We must begin to see oppositions as hurdles to climb over and as interruptions, but not as cancellations.

So when we hear the resounding question of "Why me?" within our heart, let's take a deep breath and be thankful that we have been chosen as a vessel of honor to glorify our Heavenly Father. And when it seems like the questions continue to come, partner with me and resolve that, "It is me because God said so and that's that. So be it. Amen."

Points to ponder

The dynamics may differ, but the problem is the same	weights and sin.
There are different applications but the same formula	repent, believe, receive.
There are diverse equations but the answer is the same	Jesus Christ.

He will never leave us nor forsake us.
(He hath said, I will never leave thee, nor forsake thee.
Hebrew 13:5c.)

For *This* I Thank You

Thank You, Lord, for being more to me
than I could ever be to myself.
For loving me too much to leave me the way I am.

It can be difficult to understand comments like, "the way up is down," "it is in giving that you receive," "a man can't stumble when he is on his knees." However, in the past 16 years, I'm getting the concept of these statements. I'm moving away from the "Why is this happening?" to the "How do I get through this?" And I've found that the best way to get through anything and to do it with the least amount of time and struggle is to just say *thank You*.

The circumstances may be distasteful, yet I say thank You for keeping me from becoming complacent and not continuing to pursue my destiny. Being chosen in the furnace of affliction is definitely not a fun place to be, but wherever and for whatever reason, I have found that with You, Lord, it is the safest place to be.

Thank You for when I am alone. For it is then that I know, like David, You are a present help in times of trouble. I can answer with assurance when I'm asked, "But Whom do you say I am?" that You are MY Shepherd. I know for a fact that the effectual fervent prayer of a righteous man availeth much.

Thank You for the times when I'm lonely. I find Your promises are true. You will never forsake me or leave me comfortless. You are there in the midst of it all.

Thank You when the promotion comes not. Or when the praises of man, validation or affirmation come at the *right time*, for You are helping me to make sure I do all things heartily as unto the Lord. I strive to please the One who can destroy body and soul, to seek the kingdom of God and His righteousness so that all else that I need will be added.

Thank You for the times I come to You dismayed about the successes of others who seem to prosper and have little or no regard for You. It is only when I come into Your sanctuary, Lord, that I know I desire You more than anything on earth. My health may fail and my spirit may grow weak, but *You*, God, remain the strength of my heart. You are mine forever. (Psalm 73:25, NLT)

I recall words of testimony over the years—"I thank God for life, health and strength and for keeping me from dangers, seen and unseen." I now have a deeper appreciation for those words. I see many people who have life but do not possess health and strength.

I thank You, God, for the activity of my limbs, for being clothed and in my right mind. I thank You that each member of my family is healthy and able to function by themselves.

Every day new mercies I see. Thank You for giving us this day our daily bread. Thank You for blessing our going out and our coming in. At the end of each day I thank You. When I awake during the night and hear the breathing of my spouse beside me, I thank You.

For relationships I thank You. I thank You for my fore parents who gave me the foundation of salvation and showed me the tools that would enable me to continue to build upon the Rock. Some relationships have given me positive encouragement to be all I can be, and those who weren't as positive have helped me to soar higher by showing me what I didn't want to be. I truly thank You for the ones You have planted to help me cross bridges as I get to them.

Even when I don't do everything right and I've truly blown it, I thank You for the mind to seek You, to confess my shortcomings and not give up.

It may be fire or it may be flood, I may not understand nor does it make any sense to the natural man, but Lord, I thank You for your blood which sustains me to fulfill Your purpose for my life and bring me to my expected end.

For all of this I thank You!!

Thank You for compelling me to go beyond having a form of godliness and denying the power thereof to living in the Spirit and possessing the anointing that destroys the yoke.

Thank You, Lord, that in the midst of pain and uncertainties there is a peaceful calm on the inside that surpasseth all understanding.

Thank You for forgiving me before I was even aware of my sinfulness, for providing a way of escape for me any time and every time I am tempted.

Thank You for Jesus Christ, my High Priest, who understands all things and is there as my Advocate and Mediator each time I need Him.

I thank You because I can come boldly to the throne of grace, use the access code, which is Your name, and obtain mercy and find grace to help in time of need.

Thank you for your Holy Spirit Who empowers me, teaches me and guides me,

And for being the Lover of my soul.
For this and so much more, I thank YOU!

Parent Time

Of the many things we get when we leave the hospital as new parents, we do not get a manual giving us all the details of "how to" in regard to being consistent, nurturing, loving and fun-filled parents!!

In our efforts to not be "as strict as my parents were," I sometimes think we fail to be strict enough. Few of us find where the balance is and fewer of us find that balance in time to make a difference in the early lives of our children.

I feel safe in saying that a high percentage of us grew up where there was extended family—grandparents, aunts, uncles and cousins—living in close proximity to each other and no matter what happened, we always had the support of immediate family. And we had the same basic family dynamics, values and moral principles.

However today, because of military and employment relocations, many of us are miles and miles away from family. And because of a high population of mixed culture and ethnic groups, we often do not have relationships with our neighbors or even in a close surrounding community. Some of us are part of a Christian community, but yet there are few close interpersonal relationships.

The challenges that are before us today are great. We can have rules and guidelines for our households yet the best friends of our children could be uniquely different. There are blended families, mixed cultural families, a combination of blended mixed cultures, and single parent households. It is important that parents give a sense of security at home so that no matter what children encounter with their peers at daycare, school, work or play, they will be confident in who they are and not feel the need to conform to any pressure that will put them at risk of negative consequences in their home environment.

How do we as parents find balance when the balancing scale is tilted?

I believe it starts with me, the individual parent, in knowing who I am, whose I am and my purpose of being. When I am sure of "me" I can be more cognizant of training my child in the way "he" should go. I am able to see each child as an individual *person*—one in whom God has placed seeds of potential that are unlike anyone else—for me to develop and nurture him in the fear and admonition of God.

Although the Bible is very clear about the father's role in parenting (Ephesians 6:4; Colossians 3:21), many mothers are longing for their children to see and experience the development of an intimate relationship that will remain between their children and their fathers.

How do mothers provide emotional stability that leads to spiritual enrichment when the father/child component is missing?

I believe a genuine understanding of why the father is not active in the child's life and real faith in God can help women raise children to be well-adjusted, stable Christian adults.

The Bible tells us of a lady by the name of Abi, who was married to King Ahaz, and was primarily responsible for the discipline and guidance of their son, Hezekiah. In spite of the ungodly rule of King Ahaz, when Hezekiah became king at age 25 after his father died, he led the nation in a sweeping revival (2 Kings 18).

While some mothers are single, there are many mothers whose husbands are in the military, workaholics, truck drivers or just sinful and rebellious. Some husbands are in the house, but silent. And this still makes the mother the primary role model. Today, more fathers, for various reasons, are becoming the primary caregiver. To you, I tip my hat.

As a single parent, I imagine it is a challenge to not demean the other parent in the eyes of the children. One must realize that although a husband/wife relationship may no longer exist, once we become parents, we will always be parents. Not being a good spouse does not necessarily mean that we are not or cannot be good parents.

I've had the challenge of bridging the gap between our son and his child's mother. Although they are no longer intimate, they have developed a rapport that allows them to be good parents. Our oldest daughter has two daughters and is no longer married to their father. It is an on-going adjustment in facing the challenges she confronts in meeting their needs. She works full-time; her older daughter has juvenile diabetes and the younger suffers from a respiratory disorder. The dad is remarried and lives in another state, and we grandparents live 1,000+ miles from them. Our second daughter has two children and although she and her husband live together, the challenge is still great because he is in full-time youth ministry.

Mothers, if you find yourself being the primary role model in your child's life, fret not. Your genuine faith in God can help you to raise a healthy, well-balanced, God-fearing child.

Fathers, it is never too late to bridge the gap between you and your offspring. Don't let the price be too high. It is vital to let your children see you respect their mother. You may not have an intimate love relationship with her anymore and your relationship may be estranged, but prayerfully you can see her as one of God's creations and not as an object. In many cases, all that is needed with your child is your time — time to listen (not demand), time to hug (not abuse), time to laugh (not scold), time to appreciate, (not to demean), time to say "I love you" and most of all, time to pray with them and for them.

God saw our need as His children and sacrificed His only Son so that we may have abundant life. He loved us in spite of…not because of.

I'm thankful that I was raised in a two-parent home where love and respect were shown. Godly principles, along with discipline and chastisement, were taught by word of mouth, as well as by example.

My husband, Roy, was raised in a one-parent family. Although he knew his dad, who lived in another city and later in another state, and saw him on occasions, they became closer when Roy reached adulthood. His experience was very helpful in the care and nurturing he gave to our children as they were growing up and in the way he continues to nurture them and be their friend. We were able to have a household with guidelines that allowed each person to be respected as one of God's creations. Roy and I knew that it was important for us to maintain a united front, regardless of personal opinions, for the Word warns us that a house divided against itself will not stand.

The ultimate goal of parenting is to help children successfully make the journey from childhood to mature, well-balanced adults. Good parenting is not only a challenge, but it represents years of commitment and long-term investments. It doesn't guarantee that our children will not make mistakes and choices that will be to their harm and sometimes their shame (and ours), but it assures them a solid foundation to build on and a godly standard as a guide and gauge.

Our faith in God helps us fill our children's emotional tanks with unconditional love. This love accepts and affirms a child for who he is, not for what he does. Few children feel unconditionally loved and cared for because few parents know how to transfer their heartfelt love to the hearts of their children. We must communicate love in a language they understand.

G. Chapman & R. Campbell, M.D.'s book, *The Five Love Languages of Children* explained that although each child has a primary love language, all five languages— tender touch, supporting words, quality time, gifts and acts of service—converge to meet your child's needs. Because you want your children to grow into full maturity, you will want to show them love in all the languages and then teach them how to use these for themselves.

Whatever you do, don't become discouraged and throw in the towel for a quitter never wins and a winner never quits. When in doubt, ask God for wisdom for He "giveth to all men liberally" (James 1:5) and "In all your ways acknowledge Him, and He shall direct your paths." (Proverbs 3:6) "Great peace have they which love thy law: and nothing shall offend them." (Psalm 119:165)

As a volunteer in Pastoral Care at St. Francis Hospital, one of my pleasures is to visit new moms and their babies. The hospital has provided a prayer for the parents and a blessing for the babies. I would like to take the opportunity to share this prayer with you in hope that you will be inspired and encouraged to continue in your parenting, no matter how old you and your children are. Although all of my children are grown, I find it to be inspirational whenever I feel that I need a bit more insight. Because you see, once a parent, always a parent. And it is more challenging to parent grown children than younger ones. I strive to be more respectful and to be their friend and allow God to be their "parent." I pray that you be blessed.

A PARENT'S PRAYER

Oh, Heavenly Father, make me a better parent.
Teach me to understand my children,
to listen patiently to what they have to say
and to answer all their questions kindly.
Keep me from interrupting them or contradicting them.
Make me as courteous to them
as I would have them be to me.
Forbid that I should ever laugh at their mistakes,
or resort to shame or ridicule
when they displease me.
May I never punish them for my own selfish
satisfaction or to show my power.
Let me not tempt my child to lie or steal.
Guide me hour by hour that
I may demonstrate by all I say and do
that honestly produces happiness.
When I am out of sorts, help me,
O Lord, to hold my tongue.
May I ever be mindful that my children are children
and I should not expect of them the judgment of adults.
Let me not rob them of the opportunity to wait on them-
selves and to make decisions.
Bless me with the bigness to grant them all
their reasonable requests,
and the courage to deny them privileges
I know will do them harm.
Make me fair and just and kind.
And fit me, Lord, to be loved and respected
and imitated by my children.

by Garry Myers

(Children) **Be ye followers of me** (parents)**, even as I** (parents) **also am of Christ.**
1 Corinthians 11: 1

Woman to Woman

God designed the female with a complex, emotionally charged personality that continuously changes from birth to death. Many times the only way for us to see ourselves is in the face of another female.

We are designed with such uniqueness that only God understands how to orchestrate it in our lives. We are so intricate that we can be nurturing and compassionate, yet conniving and condescending; open and vulnerable, yet reserved and withdrawn. We may even have a few love/hate relationships.

Mother to daughter, sister to sister, friend to friend, old to young, even to the women we pass on the by-ways of life, we have the capability of reaching out and touching without extending a hand. We can give a kind word without the parting of our lips. There is an unexplained instinct that allows us to give a smile, a nod and yes, sometimes a frown or just a look that says, "I understand."

As we grow from one stage to another, we encounter many challenges that can equip us to grow older gracefully or to become brass and bitter. There is a saying that states, "Growing old is inevitable, but growing up is optional." I want to grow up as I grow older. What about you?

Sometimes we are the protégée, other times we are the mentor.

When I am the protégée, I want to be teachable and open to learning. It matters not that my mentor is younger than me or if we are peers, I will respect and adhere to the wisdom that is being conveyed.

I recall when my husband and I were being challenged with the changes taking place in our life because of his accident. One person who had great impact in my life was younger than me and single, and the other one was my peer. When I am the mentor, I pray to be caring and sensitive to the person as an individual first and then relationally.

There are no set rules for mentoring. It is simply being able to counsel, guide and give support to someone who is experiencing something that God has given you insight into. That insight may be from experience or from divine revelation. It is just being able to walk with one another through a season in life.

I have gained a great deal of insight and guidance from my children. My three girls married men who were raised in one-parent households while I was raised in a two-parent home. My oldest daughter is now a divorcee with two girls. My second daughter is married to a man in ministry. My youngest *was* (she is now a born-again Christian) a strong-willed, very opinionated, street-savy rebel. And as I have encountered situations in the classroom and in out-reach ministry, my relationship with my girls is helpful in equipping me to be more open minded and effective as I teach and share.

It doesn't matter about the distance or the time spent together. It is more about quality. There is a reading titled, *A Reason, A Season, A Lifetime*. I often refer to it by saying that many people who are in my life are there in different seasons, for different reasons, throughout my lifetime.

The Serenity Prayer is very helpful to me when I am confronted with transitions within my own life and as I share with others. It is important to be aware of what can be changed and change it. What cannot be changed we must recognize and release. As I courageously and with wisdom apply these principles in my life, I can strengthen my sister. We may not have an identical situation, but many times the same principles can be applied, and it is always easier to conquer a task with someone holding your hand who has been there and done that, than it is in walking alone.

My endeavor is to allow challenges to help me be sensitive to the Holy Spirit, intuitive and compassionate to the female gender, no matter the age, race or creed, whether I am the receiver or the giver.

It may be impossible to literally touch person to person, but through pleasantness, a smile, a slight nod, direct eye contact or a gentle handshake, we can reach out to them. And when we are on bended knees we can reach out through prayer, praise and worship and send supportive hugs...

Woman to Woman

My Inspirations
From You to Me

I have shared with you many seasons that have taken place in my life. Now I will share with you some of the wonderful encouragements that I have received that have helped me to continue to press forward. When I think that I am near the breaking point or just that no one cares, God always shows up.

When my husband, Roy, was first in the accident, I thought my life was truly over, but God...

My brother, Ezra, had moved to Spokane a few years prior to the accident and I had always said that if I ever needed him, it would take him five or more hours to get to me. But on **this** day, he was here. I have no idea how — it was just by divine order. You see, he had called me from a phone booth about an hour earlier telling me goodbye and that he was getting on the freeway headed back to Spokane. But as I was seated in the holding room with the hospital chaplain, waiting for the worst news of my life, Ezra walked through the door.

There was a social gathering going on at church when I received the news and after I made a phone call back to the church, it seemed as though the entire group gathered in the emergency waiting area. Not only did they gather there, many of them went back to church for an all night prayer vigil while others stayed with me.

One Christmas when Roy had lost his job and our funds were low, we decided to share gifts from the heart. We actually celebrated Jesus' birthday by writing cards to Him and to each other. This became a tradition for us. The words that my husband gave me one year have remained very dear in my heart. The card read: *"Merry Christmas... to my wife, the love of my life. Thank you for being the person you are. The transformation in your life is wonderful."* I still have it.

It is always uplifting to go to the mailbox and come back with a card from across the United States that reads, *"A Friend is a Gift, it's never just one thing...a spirit-lifting chat, a soft shoulder, a wise word, a jewel of insight or a shared moment of laughter. It's the magical blend that is only found in a special friend like you."*

And when it seems like going to church is just another routine, but with a heart's cry of "Lord, I really need you to lift my spirit today," and the usher brings a note that begins with *"You're So Special."* Even if the rest of the reading isn't profound, the title was enough to let me know that God was looking out for "ME." However, the words that followed were just as meaningful and they were written from the heart of the sender:

"Occasionally it has to feel that no one seems to care
how you always find the time in other's needs to share.
Sometimes in the words of a card
or a message left on the phone,
other times with your physical presence
so people are not alone.
The sacrifices that you make have not been easy to do
and seldom does it provide any recognition to you;
but still you make them frequently as if it matters not,
when no kind words or gratitude is all the thanks you got.

I guess you found the secret,
that from God your blessings flow.
And whether rewards are seen or not,
He causes winds to blow.
Your faith is not in what you see
or it would have long since died,
but through the years you've come to know
your needs God has supplied."

At times when I least expect it, the Lord allows me to receive an e-mail, phone card or note, just to say *I love you.*

There have been times when I've felt like my birth children were not in tune with my needs as a person. The many times that they are, are sufficient and heart touching enough for me to know they care and they are always just a call away. There has never been a time when I needed them that they didn't come through.

Cassandra, Chelesa, Calveo and Consuella, you and yours are many of my most prized inspirations. I would not be where I am today without your love and support. You inspire me to keep moving forward and you are giving me the opportunity to share experiences that will make your life less complex.

To God be the glory for all of my "children by choice" and friends who God allows to just flow in my life. We are helpers one to another and the love and encouragement that God always shows me, I pass along to you.

The following words are from a card sent to me by Mrs. Shirley Jackson, one of my mentors who is now in her heavenly home:

20 Beautiful Things That are True About You

"You are something and someone very special. You really
are. No one else in this entire world is exactly like you and
there are so many beautiful things about you.
You're a one-of-a-kind treasure,
uniquely here in this space and time.
You are here to shine in your own wonderful way,
sharing your smile in the best way you can, and remem-
bering all the while that a little light somewhere
makes a brighter light everywhere.
You can and you do make a wonderful
contribution to this world.
You have qualities within you that many people would love
to have, and those who really
and truly know you, are so glad that they do.
You have a big heart and a good and sensitive soul.
You are gifted with thoughts and ways of seeing things
that only special people know.
You know that life doesn't always play by the rules,
but that in the long run, everything will work out.
You understand that you and your actions are capable of
turning anything around and that joys
once lost can always be found.
There is a resolve and an inner reserve of strength in you
that few ever get to see. You have so many treasures within,
those you're only beginning to discover,
and all the ones you're already aware of.
Never forget what a treasure you are.
That special person in the mirror
may not always get to hear all
the compliments you so sweetly deserve,

> *but you are so worthy of such an abundance*
> *of friendship, joy and love."*
> *Remember, weeping endures for that night*
> *but joy comes in the morning.*

Many times when I've wondered if writing is really a part of my destiny, someone will ask me about my writing. More directly, the Lord will speak to me personally and openly by an evangelist or my pastor. I recall a time when a dear friend came and ran a revival at church. He also has a prophetic ministry. He came to where I was standing, grabbed my hand and escorted me down front. One of the many things he said to me was, "You're writing a book and you already have the workings for your next one." WOW, what a surprise! I had told no one there and he and I had not seen one another in years. My response was to God, "Okay, I hear You."

In my dilemmas of "what if" and "how to" God always comes through and confirms that yes, writing is part of His plan for me. I'm constantly being put in touch with people who know this person or that one who does this or that. One Sunday after church one of my church peers offered her services to edit.

In the summer of 2005, while spending time with one of my daughters and her children, my eldest granddaughter gave me a bracelet that reads, *realize your dream.*

When all else fails to convince me, God speaks to me through daily devotions. One of the latest ones is from Psalm 102:18, This will be written for the generations to come. That a people yet to be created may praise the Lord (NKJV). The heading read, "Write what the Lord has done." The commentator encouraged the readers to pass on to their loved ones how God had helped them overcome problems and fulfill His purposes through their lives.

As I have procrastinated in getting this book published (it has been written for more than two years), one of my nieces gave me a CD that spoke of family legacy. The speaker was challenged by his daughter to write the book that was within him so as to release the book (s) within her. He said even if his book sat on the back shelf of a book close-out, he had to write. I thought of my son who is a poet within his own right. He would often say to me, "I will follow in your foot-steps." And since my desire for our children is for them to reach their highest potential, my steps must be onward and upward. The higher I climb the fewer steps they will have to make.

Not only for my children and my grandchildren, but as my niece encouraged me, future generations will have the opportunity to see glimpses of their rich legacy! This book will be to them a modern day testament of Who God is, affirming the fact that He is the same yesterday, today and forever. He is a God Who always comes through.

And just as He encourages me, I know He'll do the same for you. He is not a God Who is a respecter of persons. I exhort you to continue in your pursuit of your dreams, keep your heart in tune because I know He speaks. The question is, "How well are we listening?"

Listen with your whole being—your body, your soul and your spirit. He speaks in most unusual ways and when we least expect it. One day when paying a bill after having lunch with a friend, I looked up and saw a picture that had this reading beneath it, "Always follow your dream." This is also the day that the Lord solidified the title of this book through my friend.

Each of you encouraged me to never give up,
to alwayssss

folloooow

GOD!

Epilog

God has given us a road map, the Bible, which will ensure us a safe journey from earth to glory. It is up to us to read it, study it and follow it's route. If you have never been to my house, why would you second-guess the directions that I have given you? So, since we've not been to Heaven, why do we think that we can get there with our own choosing?

When we accept Jesus Christ as our Savior *and* Lord, we are to seek those things above where Christ is seated on the right hand of God. Our affections are to be set on things above and not on things of this earth. We are to think it not strange when fiery trials come our way because satan is as a roaring lion, walking to and fro, seeking whom he may devour. His weapons are in many forms, but when we are dressed in the whole armor of God, we are protected from the wiles of the enemy and no weapon formed against us will prosper.

As we look to the hills from whence cometh our help and know the character of God, we will remember that Jesus fought and won the war for us and we are more than conquerors. So when we show up to fight in every battle, we can be confident that these light afflictions are nothing in comparison to eternal glory. *Praise God!!!*

It may seem as though the more determined we are to live in confident faith, the more battles we are confronted with…but God.

I wish I could say that my life is peaches and cream, but I can't. However, I can say that it is a bed of roses — it has beauty, fragrance and *thorns*. And when I'm not careful with my approach, I can be stuck with an unexpected prick. And again…but God.

I won't bore you with the many things I'm continually challenged with. I'll just tell you that I know from whence my help comes and that He is able to keep everything that I commit to Him against *any day*. I've learned to seek His face and not His hand. I enjoy my time with Him for Who He is and not just for what He does. When I am weak, He is strong. I've placed an altar-like picturesque in our home to help remind us of the continual presence of Almighty God.

In times of weakness, despair, and yes, even sin, we can be strong because we have all-the-time access to His throne. Jesus Christ, our Advocate and Mediator, is always there and we can approach the Most Holy Place boldly and find grace in times of need. We have the Holy Spirit as our gift to empower us, teach us, guide us and comfort us. The weak can say they are strong and when we are strong, we can help to strengthen our brethren.

We are sojourners passing through this barren land on our way to our heavenly home, and as we look to the "I AM" in our everyday situations and are faithful unto Him, we shall be blessed and come forth as pure gold.

From me to YOU…

Be Strengthened…

Be Encouraged…

Continually.

Man's True Best Friend

I remember as a child hearing you say that there was no
charge for the nine months you carried me and to this day
your prayers are still pulling me through.
We have been through some tough times as a family where
you had to take on the role of dad too,
now it`s my turn as I cry and type to say
that I`m proud of YOU!
You have stood in the gap for us when things were going
wrong and people had started to count
our family down and out,
but it was your prayer life and connection with GOD that
helped to show others what FAMILY was really all about.
I`m thirty seven years old now and in my life a lot of
people have come and gone,
but you have become a Best Friend to me
and encourages me to be strong.
I don`t know what I`d do without you in my life but I know
one thing that you would say, God is the Source of all your
strength and He is only a prayer away.
I`m praying for you as son to mom and friend to friend, for
all the things you still see and pray me through;
a shoulder to cry on, a smile to see
as this Man's Best Friend.
I Love you.
From Me to YOU! 🌹 Your son, DeWayne.

133

Printed in the United States
129591LV00005B/4-18/P